ExpressWays

ENGLISH FOR COMMUNICATION

1

Steven J. Molinsky · Bill Bliss

 PRENTICE HALL REGENTS, Englewood Cliffs, NJ 07632

Library of Congress Cataloging-in-Publication Data
(Revised for vol. 1)

Molinsky, Steven J.
  ExpressWays : English for communication.

  Includes indexes.
  1. English language—Text-books for foreign speakers.
I. Bliss, Bill.   II. Title.
PE1128.M674   1986   428.3′4   85-30059
ISBN 0-13-298423-7 (v. 1)

Editorial/production supervision and
  interior design: Sylvia Moore
Development: Ellen Lehrburger
Cover design: Lundgren Graphics, Ltd.
Manufacturing buyer: Lorraine Fumoso
Page layout: Diane Koromhas

Illustrations and cover drawing by Gabriel Polonsky

© 1988 by Prentice-Hall, Inc.
A Simon & Schuster Company
Englewood Cliffs, New Jersey 07632

Printed in the United States of America

10 9 8 7

ISBN 0-13-298423-7

Prentice-Hall International (UK) Limited, *London*
Prentice-Hall of Australia Pty. Limited, *Sydney*
Prentice-Hall Canada Inc., *Toronto*
Prentice-Hall Hispanoamericana, S.A., *Mexico*
Prentice-Hall of India Private Limited, *New Delhi*
Prentice-Hall of Japan, Inc., *Tokyo*
Prentice-Hall of Southeast Asia Pte. Ltd., *Singapore*
Editora Prentice-Hall do Brasil, Ltda., *Rio de Janeiro*

ii

Contents

Singular/Plural • Prepositions of Location • Adjectives
• Too + Adjective • Ordinal Numbers • Want to
• Question Formation

Want-Desire • Directions-Location • Satisfaction/Dissatisfaction
• Attracting Attention • Gratitude
• Checking and Indicating Understanding • Hesitating

TO THE TEACHER

ExpressWays is a functional English program for adult and young-adult learners of English. The program consists of the following components:

Student Course Books—offering intensive conversational practice;
Companion Workbooks—offering grammar, reading, writing, and listening comprehension practice fully coordinated with the student course books;
Guide Books—providing background notes and expansion activities for all lessons and step-by-step instructions for teachers;
Audio Program—offering realistic presentation of dialogs in the texts;
Picture Program—including Picture Cards for vocabulary development and Dialog Visual Cards that depict scenes and characters from the texts;
Placement and Achievement Testing Program—providing tools for the evaluation of student levels and progress.

ExpressWays—Book 1 is intended for adult and young-adult students of English at the beginning level. The text provides an introduction to basic grammar and vocabulary and the usage of English for everyday life situations. *ExpressWays—Book 1* is organized by topics, or competencies, while incorporating integrated coverage of functions and beginning-level grammar.*

THE DIMENSIONS OF COMMUNICATION: FUNCTION, FORM, AND CONTENT

A number of texts present a "topical," or competency-based, syllabus by covering vocabulary items and key expressions needed for specific situations. A number of other texts present a "functional" syllabus by describing language use and listing sets of functional phrases. In both cases, texts tend to focus exclusively on the one dimension of communication that organizes the syllabus. In addition, both topical and functional texts do not usually give students intensive communicative practice using the correct grammatical forms that are required by particular key expressions or functional language choices.

---

* *ExpressWays—Books 1 and 2* are organized by a spiralled curriculum. They are based on a core topical curriculum that is covered at different degrees of intensity and depth at each level. *ExpressWays—Book 1* provides students with the most important vocabulary, grammar, and functional expressions needed to communicate at a basic level in a full range of situations and contexts. *ExpressWays—Book 2* covers the same full range of situations and contexts, but offers students expanded vocabulary, more complex grammar, and a wider choice of functional expressions.

ExpressWays—Book 3 is organized by functions, while incorporating integrated coverage of higher level topics and grammar. *ExpressWays—Foundations* is a simplified edition of Book 1, for students who require more basic material and who perhaps have more limited reading and writing skills.

ExpressWays—Book 1 aims to provide dynamic, communicative practice that involves students in lively interactions based on the content of real-life contexts and situations. The topically organized syllabus is fully integrated into a complete conversational course in which students not only learn the vocabulary and expressions needed for essential life situations, but also learn the various ways to express the functions of English and intensively practice the grammatical forms required to competently produce these expressions and functions.

Every lesson in the program offers students simultaneous practice with one or more functions, the grammatical forms needed to express those functions, and the contexts and situations in which the functions and grammar are used. This "tri-dimensional clustering" of function, form, and content is the organizing principle behind each lesson and the cornerstone of the *ExpressWays* approach to functional syllabus design.

ExpressWays aims to offer students broad exposure to uses of language in a variety of relevant contexts: in community, academic, employment, home, and social settings. The characters portrayed are people of different ages, ethnic groups, and occupations, interacting in real-life situations.

While some texts make a point of giving students a range of ways of expressing a function, from extremely polite to very impolite, we have chosen to "take the middle ground" and concentrate on those expressions that would most frequently occur in normal polite conversation between people in various settings. *ExpressWays* does offer a variety of registers, from the formal language someone might use in a job interview, with a customer, or when speaking with an authority figure, to the informal language someone would use when talking with family members, co-workers, or friends.

A special feature of the program is the treatment of discourse strategies. Students actively practice initiating conversations and topics, hesitating, checking and indicating understanding, and other conversation skills.

AN OVERVIEW

Guided Conversations

Guided Conversations are the dialogs and exercises that are the central learning devices in the program. Each lesson begins with a model guided conversation that depicts a real-life situation and the vocabulary, grammar, and functions used in the communication exchange. In the exercises that follow, students create new conversations by placing new contexts, content, or characters into the framework of the model.

"Now Present Your Own Conversations"

Each lesson ends with this open-ended exercise which offers students the opportunity to create and present original conversations based on the model. Students contribute content based on their experiences, ideas, and imaginations, while staying within the framework of the model.

We should emphasize that the objective of each lesson is to provide a measure of controlled practice with a dialog and guided conversation exercises so that students can competently create their own, original conversations.

Interchange

This end-of-chapter activity offers students the opportunity to create and present "guided role plays." Each activity consists of a model that students can practice and then use as a basis for their original presentations. Students should be encouraged to be inventive and to use new vocabulary in these presentations and should feel free to adapt and expand the model any way they wish.

Scenes & Improvisations

These "free role plays" appear after every third chapter, offering review and synthesis of lessons in the three preceding chapters. Students are presented with eight scenes depicting conversations between people in various situations. They use the information in the scenes to determine who the people are and what they are talking about. Then, students improvise based on their perceptions of the scenes' characters, contexts, and situations.

The purpose of these improvisations is to offer free recombination practice that promotes students' absorption of the preceding chapters' vocabulary, grammar, and functions into their repertoire of active language use.

Support and Reference Sections

ExpressWays offers a number of support and reference sections:

- *Chapter Opening Pages* provide an overview of topics, grammar, and key functions and conversation strategies highlighted in each chapter.
- *End-of-Chapter Summaries* provide complete lists of topic vocabulary and grammar structures appearing in each chapter.
- A *Chapter-by-Chapter Summary of Functions and Conversation Strategies* in the Appendix provides an overview of all expressions for the functions and conversation strategies in each chapter.
- A *Topic Vocabulary Glossary* provides a listing of key vocabulary domains included in the text and indicates the pages where the words first appear.
- An *Index of Functions and Conversation Strategies*, an *Index of Topics* and an *Index of Grammatical Structures* provide a convenient reference for locating coverage of functions, topics, and grammar in the text.

THE TOTAL *ExpressWays* PROGRAM

The *ExpressWays Student Course Books* are essentially designed to offer intensive communicative practice. These texts may be used independently, or in conjunction with the *ExpressWays Companion Workbooks*, which offer practice in the other skill areas of reading, writing, and listening, as well as focused practice with particular grammar structures as they occur in the program. Each exercise in the Companion Workbook indicates the specific Student Course Book page that it corresponds to.

The *ExpressWays Guide Books* provide step-by-step instructions for coverage of each lesson, background notes, sample answers to guided conversation exercises, and answer keys and listening-activity scripts for exercises in the Companion Workbooks. For teachers of multi-level classes, the Guide Books indicate for each lesson the corresponding page in *ExpressWays—Foundations* that covers the same topic at a lower level, and the corresponding page in *ExpressWays—Book 2* that covers the same topic at a higher level.

Perhaps the most important feature of the Guide Books is the expansion exercise that is recommended for each lesson. These exercises offer students free, spontaneous practice with the vocabulary, grammar, and functions that are presented in the Student Course Books. Activities include improvisations, "information gap" role plays, problem-solving, and topics for discussion and debate. We encourage teachers to use these activities or similar ones as springboards to help their students "break away" from the text and incorporate lesson content into their everyday use of English.

The *ExpressWays Audio Program* includes a set of tapes providing realistic presentation of all model dialogs and selected guided conversation exercises in the Student Course Books. The tapes are designed to be used interactively, so that the recorded voice serves as the student's speaking partner, making conversation practice possible even when the student is studying alone. The Audio Program also includes a set of tapes for the listening comprehension exercises in the Companion Workbooks.

The *ExpressWays Picture Program* includes Dialog Visual Cards and Picture Cards. The *ExpressWays Dialog Visual Cards* are poster-size illustrations depicting the characters and settings of all model dialogs. Their use during introduction of the model helps to assure that students are engaged in active listening and speaking practice during this important stage in the lesson. The *ExpressWays Picture Cards* illustrate key concepts and vocabulary items. They can be used for introduction of new material, for review, for enrichment exercises, and for role-playing activities.

The *ExpressWays Testing Program* includes a Placement Testing Kit for initial evaluation and leveling of students, and sets of Mid-Term and Final Examinations to measure students' achievement at each level of the program. All tests in the program include both oral and written evaluation components.

SUGGESTED TEACHING STRATEGIES

In using *ExpressWays*, we encourage you to develop approaches and strategies that are compatible with your own teaching style and the needs and abilities of your students. While the program does not require any specific method or technique in order to be used effectively, you may find it helpful to review and try out some of the following suggestions. (Specific step-by-step instructions may be found in the Guide Books.)

Guided Conversations

1. *Setting the Scene.* Have students look at the model illustration in the book or on the *ExpressWays* Dialog Visual Card. Set the scene: Who are the people? What is the situation?
2. *Listening to the Model.* With books closed, have students listen to the model conversation—presented by you, a pair of students, or on the audio tape.
3. *Class Practice.* With books still closed, model each line and have the whole class repeat in unison.
4. *Reading.* With books open, have students follow along as two students present the model.

   (At this point, ask students if they have any questions and check understanding of new vocabulary. You may also want to call students' attention to any related language or culture notes, which can be found in the Guide Book.)
5. *Pair Practice.* In pairs, have students practice the model conversation.
6. *Exercise Practice.* (optional) Have pairs of students simultaneously practice all the exercises.
7. *Exercise Presentations.* Call on pairs of students to present the exercises.

   (At this point, you may want to discuss any language or culture notes related to the exercises, as indicated in the Guide Book.)

"Now Present Your Own Conversations"

In these activities that follow the guided conversations at the end of each lesson, have pairs of students create and present original conversations based on the model. Encourage students to be inventive as they create their characters and situations. (You may want to assign this exercise as homework, having students prepare their original conversations, practice them the next day with another student, and then present them to the class.) In this way, students can review the previous day's lesson without actually having to repeat the specific exercises already covered.

Expansion

We encourage you to use the expansion activity for each lesson suggested in the Guide Book or a similar activity that provides students with free, spontaneous practice while synthesizing the content of the lesson.

Interchange

Have students practice the model using the same steps listed above for guided conversations. (You might want to eliminate the *Class Practice* step in the case of longer Interchange dialogs.) After practicing the model, have pairs of students create and present original conversations using the model dialog as a guide. Encourage students to be inventive and to use new vocabulary. (You may want to assign this exercise as homework, having students prepare their own conversations, practice them the next day with another student, and then present them to the class.) Students should present their conversations without referring to the written text, but they should also not memorize them. Rather, they should feel free to adapt and expand them any way they wish.

Scenes & Improvisations

Have students talk about the people and the situations, and then present role plays based on the scenes. Students may refer back to previous lessons as a resource, but they should not simply re-use specific conversations. (You may want to assign these exercises as written homework, having students prepare their conversations, practice them the next day with another student, and then present them to the class.)

Multi-Level Classes

Teachers of multi-level classes may wish to modify some of the teaching suggestions mentioned above. For example, teachers who have their students do simultaneous pair practice can have students at lower levels practice fewer exercises while students at higher levels practice more or all exercises. During this pair practice, the teacher can offer special help to students at lower levels and perhaps tell them which particular exercise they should prepare for presentation to the class.

For multi-level classes with an exceptionally wide range of ability levels, the *ExpressWays—Book 1 Guide Books* indicate for each lesson the corresponding page in *ExpressWays—Foundations* that covers the same topic at a lower level and the corresponding page in *ExpressWays—Book 2* that covers the same topic at a higher level.

In conclusion, we have attempted to offer students a communicative, meaningful, and lively way of practicing the vocabulary, grammar, and functions of English. While conveying to you the substance of our textbook, we hope that we have also conveyed the spirit: that learning to communicate in English can be genuinely interactive . . . truly relevant to our students' lives . . . and fun!

Steven J. Molinsky
Bill Bliss

Components of an ExpressWays Lesson

A **model conversation** offers initial practice with the functions and structures of the lesson.

In the **exercises**, students create conversations by placing new contexts, content, or characters into the model.

The **open-ended exercise** at the end of each lesson asks students to create and present original conversations based on the model.

Examples:

Exercise 1:

A. Excuse me. Does this train go to Brooklyn?
B. No, it doesn't. It goes to the Bronx.
A. Oh, I see. Tell me, which train goes to Brooklyn?
B. The "D" Train.
A. Thanks very much.

Exercise 2:

A. Excuse me. Does this plane go to San Francisco?
B. No, it doesn't. It goes to San Diego.
A. Oh, I see. Tell me, which plane goes to San Francisco?
B. Flight 64.
A. Thanks very much.

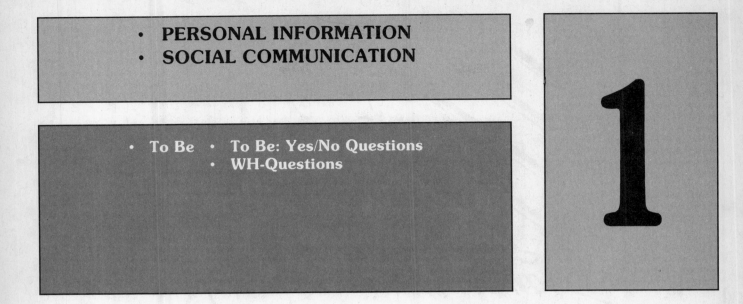

- **PERSONAL INFORMATION**
- **SOCIAL COMMUNICATION**

- To Be
- To Be: Yes/No Questions
- WH-Questions

1

Hello
I'd Like to Introduce . . .
What's Your Last Name?
What's Your Address?
Where Are You From?
Nice to Meet You

- Greeting People • Introductions
- Asking for and Reporting Information

Hello

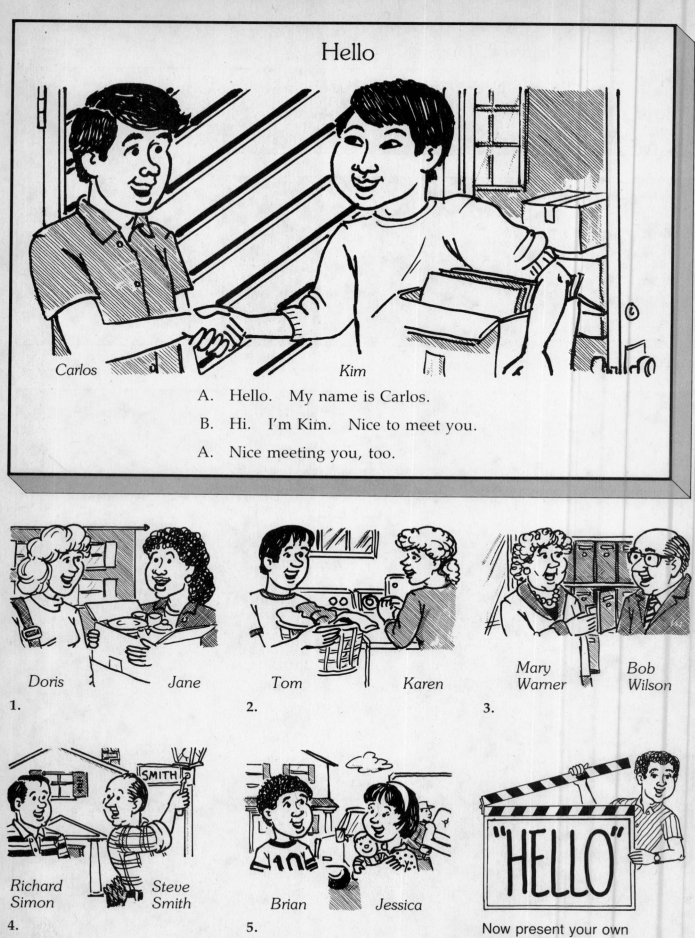

Carlos　　　　Kim

A. Hello. My name is Carlos.

B. Hi. I'm Kim. Nice to meet you.

A. Nice meeting you, too.

Doris　　　Jane

Tom　　　Karen

Mary Warner　　　Bob Wilson

1.

2.

3.

Richard Simon　　　Steve Smith

Brian　　　Jessica

"HELLO"

4.

5.

Now present your own conversations.

I'd Like to Introduce . . .

my husband, Michael

A. Hi! How are you?

B. Fine. And you?

A. Fine, thanks. I'd like to introduce you to my husband, Michael.

B. Nice to meet you.

1. my wife, Barbara

2. my father, Mr. Peterson

3. my mother, Mrs. Chen

4. my brother, George

5. my sister, Irene

Now present your own conversations.

What's Your Last Name?

Maria Sanchez

A. What's your last name?

B. Sanchez.

A. Could you spell that, please?

B. S-A-N-C-H-E-Z.

A. And your first name?

B. Maria.

1. John Clayton

2. Nancy Brenner

3. Linda Kwan

4. Robert Kelton

5. Lefty Grimes

Now present your own conversations.

What's Your Address?

10 Main Street
423-6978

A. What's your address?

B. 10 Main Street.

A. And your telephone number?

B. 423-6978.

1. 5 Summer Street
531-7624

2. 7 Pond Road
899-3263

3. 14 Maple Avenue
475-1182

4. 19 Howard Road
542-7306*

5. 1813† Central Avenue
733-8920

Now present your own
conversations.

*   0 = "oh"
†   1813 = eighteen thirteen

Where Are You From?

A. What's your name?

B. Kenji.

A. Where are you from?

B. Japan.

A. Oh. Are you from Tokyo?

B. No. I'm from Osaka.

1. Maria
   Italy

2. Hector
   Mexico

3. Mohammed
   Egypt

4. Anna
   The Soviet Union

5. Mei Ling
   China

Now present your own conversations.

INTERCHANGE
Nice to Meet You

A. Hello. My name is Franco Rossi.

B. Hello. I'm Harry Miller.

A. Are you American?

B. Yes, I am. I'm from New York.
How about you?

A. I'm Italian. I'm from Rome.

B. Nice to meet you.

A. Nice meeting you, too.

Franco Rossi	Harry Miller
Italian	American
Rome	New York

1. Carol Williams   Carmen Lopez
Canadian   Mexican
Toronto   Mexico City

2. Charles Whitmore   Ali Hassan
British   Egyptian
London   Cairo

3. David Clarke   Asako Tanaka
Australian   Japanese
Melbourne   Tokyo

4. Rick Starlight   Natasha Markova
American   Russian
Hollywood   Moscow

You're an airplane passenger on an international flight. Create an original conversation using the model dialog above as a guide. Feel free to adapt and expand the model any way you wish.

CHAPTER 1 SUMMARY

Topic Vocabulary

Personal Information	Family Members	Countries	Nationalities
name	husband	China	American
last name	wife	Egypt	Australian
first name	father	Italy	British
address	mother	Japan	Canadian
street	brother	Mexico	Egyptian
road	sister	The Soviet Union	Italian
avenue			Japanese
telephone number			Mexican
			Russian

Grammar

To Be

My name **is** Carlos.
I'm Kim.
I'm from Osaka.
I'm Italian.

To Be: Yes/No Questions

Are you from Tokyo?
Yes, I **am.**

WH-Questions

What's your name?
Where are you from?

Cardinal Numbers: 1–19

1	one	11	eleven
2	two	12	twelve
3	three	13	thirteen
4	four	14	fourteen
5	five	15	fifteen
6	six	16	sixteen
7	seven	17	seventeen
8	eight	18	eighteen
9	nine	19	nineteen
10	ten		

Functions and Conversation Strategies in this chapter are listed in the Appendix, page 193.

• TELEPHONE • GETTING AROUND TOWN
• SOCIAL COMMUNICATION

• Subject Pronouns • To Be: Am/Is/Are
• To Be: Yes/No Questions
• To Be: Negative Sentences
• Present Continuous Tense • Possessive Adjectives
• WH-Questions

I'd Like the Number of Mary Nielson
I'm Sorry. You Have the Wrong Number
Is Peter There?
Where Are You Going?
What Are You Doing?
I Can't Talk Right Now. I'm Taking a Shower

• Asking for and Reporting Information • Greeting People
• Identifying • Leave Taking

I'd Like the Number of Mary Nielson

Chicago
Mary Nielson
Hudson Avenue

863-4227

A. Directory assistance. What city?

B. Chicago. I'd like the number of Mary Nielson.

A. How do you spell that?

B. N-I-E-L-S-O-N.

A. What street?

B. Hudson Avenue.

A. Just a moment . . . The number is 863-4227.

San Francisco
Roger Craven
Day Street

1. 968-3135

New York
Connie Sato
Amsterdam Avenue

2. 747-6360

Miami
Donald Ingalls
Harbor Drive

3. 237-8044

San Antonio
Alan Kolowitz
Broadway

4. 328-1191

Philadelphia
Sally Hicks
Temple Road

5. 623-7575

"I'D LIKE THE NUMBER OF MARY NIELSON"

Now present your own conversations.

I'm Sorry. You Have the Wrong Number

A. Hello.

B. Hello, Fred?

A. I'm sorry.   You have the wrong number.

B. Is this 328-7178?

A. No, it isn't.

B. Oh.   Sorry.

1.

2.

3.

4.

5.

Now present your own conversations.

Is Peter There?

the supermarket

Peter?

Mike

the bank

Janet?

Patty

the library

Timmy and Billy?

Bobby

A. Hello. This is Mike. Is Peter there?

B. No, he isn't. He's at the supermarket.

A. Oh, I see. I'll call back later. Thank you.

A. Hello. This is Patty. Is Janet there?

B. No, she isn't. She's at the bank.

A. Oh, I see. I'll call back later. Thank you.

A. Hello. This is Bobby. Are Timmy and Billy there?

B. No, they aren't. They're at the library.

A. Oh, I see. I'll call back later. Thank you.

the post office

Fred?

Judy

1.

the laundromat

Susan?

Tim

2.

the clinic

your parents?

Mrs. Gold

3.

the park

Nancy?

Alice

4.

school

Hector?

George

5.

"IS PETER THERE?"

Now present your own conversations.

Where Are You Going?

the post office

the library

A. Hi! How are you today?

B. Fine. And you?

A. Fine, thanks. Where are you going?

B. To the library. How about you?

A. I'm going to the post office.

B. Well, nice seeing you.

A. Nice seeing you, too.

the clinic

the bank

1.

school

the supermarket

2.

the museum

the park

3.

the mall

the movies

4.

the airport

the zoo

5.

"WHERE ARE YOU GOING?"

Now present your own conversations.

What Are You Doing?

A. What are you doing?

B. I'm fixing my car.

A. What's Linda doing?

B. She's studying.

A. What's John doing?

B. He's cleaning the garage.

A. What are you doing?

B. We're doing our homework.

1. Richard
fixing his bicycle

2. you
making breakfast

3. Jennifer and Melissa
cleaning their room

4. Kevin
dancing

5. Miss Henderson
looking for her contact lens

Now present your own conversations.

INTERCHANGE
I Can't Talk Right Now. I'm Taking a Shower

A. Hello, Steve?   This is Jackie.

B. Hi.   How are you doing?

A. Pretty good.   How about you?

B. Okay.   Listen, I can't talk right now. I'm taking a shower.

A. Oh, okay.   I'll call back later.

B. Speak to you soon.

A. Good-bye.

Jackie

Steve

taking a shower

Jeff   *Pamela*

1. studying

Beth   *Debbie*

2. eating lunch

Paul   *Glen*

3. cooking dinner

Gloria   *Kathy*

4. feeding the baby

A friend is calling you on the telephone, but you can't talk right now.   Create an original conversation using the model dialog above as a guide.   Feel free to adapt and expand the model any way you wish.

CHAPTER 2 SUMMARY

Topic Vocabulary

Community

airport
bank
clinic
laundromat
library
mall
movies (movie theater)
museum
park
post office
school
supermarket
zoo

Everyday Activities

cleaning (my) room
cleaning the garage
cooking dinner
doing (my) homework
eating lunch
feeding the baby
fixing (my) bicycle
fixing (my) car
making breakfast
studying
taking a shower

Telephone

directory assistance
number

Family Members

baby
parents

Grammar

Subject Pronouns

I	I'm sorry.
he	He's at the supermarket.
she	She's at the bank.
it	No, it isn't.
we	We're doing our homework.
you	How are you today?
they	They're at the library.

To Be: Am/Is/Are

I am	I'm going to the post office.
he is	Is Peter there?
she is	Is Janet there?
it is	Is this 328-7178?
we are	We're doing our homework.
you are	Where are you going?
they are	Are Timmy and Billy there?

To Be: Yes/No Questions

Is this 328-7178?
Are Timmy and Billy there?

To Be: Negative Sentences

No, he isn't.
No, she isn't.
No, it isn't.
No, they aren't.

Present Continuous Tense

What is he doing?
What is she doing?
What are you doing?
What are they doing?

I'm fixing my car.
He's cleaning the garage.
She's studying.
We're doing our homework.
They're watching TV.

Possessive Adjectives

my	I'm fixing my car.
his	He's fixing his bicycle.
her	She's looking for her contact lens.
our	We're doing our homework.
your	What's your name?
their	They're cleaning their room.

WH-Questions

What are you doing?
Where are you going?
How do you spell that?

Functions and Conversation Strategies in this chapter are listed in the Appendix, page 193.

• GETTING AROUND TOWN
• TRANSPORTATION

• There Is • Prepositions of Location
• Simple Present Tense
• Simple Present Tense vs. To Be • Short Answers
• Imperatives • WH-Questions

Is There a Post Office Nearby?
Does This Bus Go to Westville?
Is This Bus Number 42?
Can You Tell Me How to Get to the Bus Station?
Can You Please Tell Me How to Get to the Museum?
Can You Tell Me How to Get to
Franklin's Department Store?
Excuse Me. I'm Lost

• Directions—Location • Asking for and Reporting Information
• Attracting Attention • Gratitude
• Checking and Indicating Understanding • Asking for Repetition

Is There a Post Office Nearby?

A. Excuse me. Is there a post office nearby?

B. Yes. There's a post office on Main Street.

A. On Main Street?

B. Yes. It's on Main Street, next to the bank.

A. Thank you.

A. Excuse me. Is there a laundromat nearby?

B. Yes. There's a laundromat on Grand Avenue.

A. On Grand Avenue?

B. Yes. It's on Grand Avenue, across from the bus station.

A. Thanks.

A. Excuse me. Is there a drug store nearby?

B. Yes. There's a drug store on River Street.

A. On River Street?

B. Yes. It's on River Street, between the library and the clinic.

A. Thanks very much.

A. Excuse me. Is there a supermarket nearby?

B. Yes. There's a supermarket on Davis Boulevard.

A. On Davis Boulevard?

B. Yes. It's on Davis Boulevard, around the corner from the movie theater.

A. Thank you very much.

1. hotel?

2. parking lot?

3. grocery store?

4. gas station?

5. park?

6. clinic?

7. bank?

Now present your own conversations.

19

Does This Bus Go to Westville?

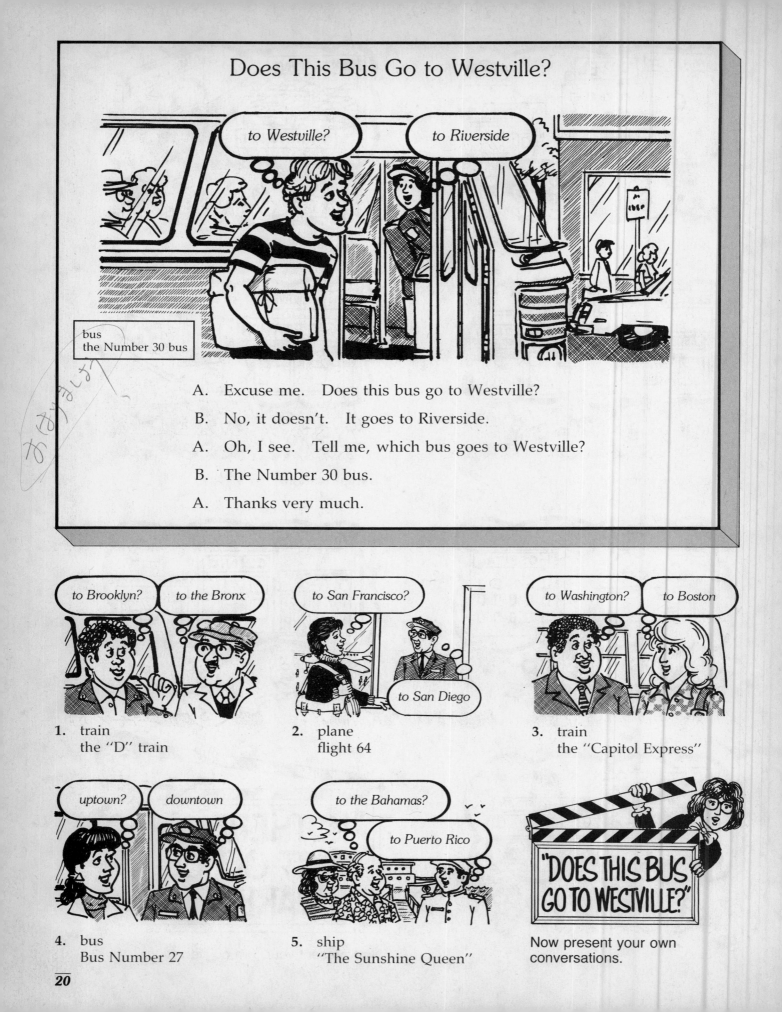

A. Excuse me. Does this bus go to Westville?

B. No, it doesn't. It goes to Riverside.

A. Oh, I see. Tell me, which bus goes to Westville?

B. The Number 30 bus.

A. Thanks very much.

1. train
   the "D" train

2. plane
   flight 64

3. train
   the "Capitol Express"

4. bus
   Bus Number 27

5. ship
   "The Sunshine Queen"

Now present your own conversations.

Is This Bus Number 42?

A. Is this Bus Number 42?
B. Yes, it is.
A. Oh, good! I'm on the right bus!

A. Is this the "F" train?
B. No, it isn't.
A. Oops! I'm on the wrong train!

A. Does this bus stop at Center Street?
B. Yes, it does.
A. Oh, good! I'm on the right bus!

A. Does this plane go to Florida?
B. No, it doesn't.
A. Oops! I'm on the wrong plane!

1.
2.
3.
4.
5.

Now present your own conversations.

Can You Tell Me How to Get to the Bus Station?

A. Excuse me. Can you tell me how to get to the bus station?

B. Yes. Walk THAT way. The bus station is on the left, next to the post office.

A. I'm sorry. Could you please repeat that?

B. All right. Walk THAT way. The bus station is on the left, next to the post office.

A. Thank you.

1.

2.

3.

4.

5.

Now present your own conversations.

Can You Please Tell Me How to Get to the Museum?

A. Excuse me. Can you please tell me how to get to the museum?

B. Yes. Walk that way to Second Avenue and turn right.

A. Uh-húh.

B. Then, go two blocks to Grove Street.

A. Okay.

B. Then, turn left on Grove Street and look for the museum on the right. Have you got that?

A. Yes. Thank you very much.

1.

2.

3.

Now present your own conversations.

Can You Tell Me How to Get to Franklin's Department Store?

A. Excuse me. Can you tell me how to get to Franklin's Department Store?

B. Sure. Take the Second Avenue bus and get off at Park Street.

A. I'm sorry. Did you say the Second Avenue bus?

B. Yes. That's right.

A. And WHERE do I get off?

B. At Park Street.

A. Thanks very much.

1.

the Metro Clinic?

the Main Street bus
Central Avenue

2.

the Regency Theater?

the Number 7 train
Broadway

3.

the science museum?

the Red Line
Grove Street

4.

City Hospital?

Bus Number 9
Harrison Road

5.

Riverside Park?

the Parkview bus
Wilson Avenue

"CAN YOU TELL ME HOW TO GET TO FRANKLIN'S DEPARTMENT STORE?"

Now present your own conversations.

Excuse Me. I'm Lost

A. Excuse me. I'm lost. Can you possibly tell me how to get to the Holiday Hotel?

B. Sure. Drive that way two miles. Then, take the West Side Expressway and get off at Exit 14. Okay so far?

A. Yes. I'm following you.

B. Then, turn right at Grand Avenue and look for the Holiday Hotel on the left. Have you got that?

A. Yes. I understand. Thanks very much.

A. Excuse me. I'm lost. Can you possibly tell me how to get to _____?

B. Sure. _____.
   Then, _____. Okay so far?

A. Yes. I'm following you.

B. Then, _____.
   Have you got that?

A. Yes. I understand. Thanks very much.

You're going somewhere by car, by public transportation, or on foot . . . and you're lost! Ask someone for directions. Create an original conversation using the model dialog above as a guide. Feel free to adapt and expand the model any way you wish.

Topic Vocabulary

Community

bank
bus station
clinic
department store
drug store
fire station
gas station
grocery store
hospital
hotel
laundromat
library
movie theater
museum
park
parking lot
police station
post office
shopping mall
supermarket
theater
train station

Transportation

boat
bus
plane
ship
train

expressway
exit

Grammar

There is

Is there a post office nearby?
There's a post office on Main Street.

Prepositions of Location

It's **on** Main Street.
It's **next to** the bank.
It's **across from** the bus station.
It's **between** the library and the clinic.
It's **around the corner from** the movie theater.

Simple Present Tense

Does this bus go to Westville?
No, it **doesn't.**

It **goes** to Riverside.

Simple Present Tense vs. To Be

Is this Bus Number 42?
Yes, it **is.**
No, it **isn't.**

Does this bus stop at Center Street?
Yes, it **does.**
No, it **doesn't.**

Short Answers

Yes, it is.
No, it isn't.

Yes, it does.
No, it doesn't.

Imperatives

Walk that way to Second Avenue.

WH-Questions

Which bus goes to Westville?

Cardinal Numbers: 20–99

20   twenty
21   twenty-one
22   twenty-two
23   twenty-three
•   •
•   •
29   twenty-nine
30   thirty
40   forty
50   fifty
60   sixty
70   seventy
80   eighty
90   ninety
99   ninety-nine

Ordinal Numbers: 1st–5th

1st   first
2nd   second
3rd   third
4th   fourth
5th   fifth

Functions and Conversation Strategies in this chapter are listed in the Appendix, pages 193–194.

SCENES & IMPROVISATIONS
Chapters 1, 2, 3

Who do you think these people are?
What do you think they're talking about?
Create conversations based on these scenes and act them out.

1.

2.

3.

4.

5.

6.

7.

8.

• Singular/Plural • Count/Non-Count Nouns
• This/That/These/Those • There Is/There Are
• Articles: A/An • Article: The • Some/Any
• Imperatives • Have/Has
• Simple Present Tense vs. To Be

We're Looking for a Two-Bedroom
Apartment Downtown
Is There a Refrigerator in the Kitchen?
How Much Is the Rent?
Where Do You Want This Sofa?
There Aren't Any More Cookies
There Isn't Any More Milk
Excuse Me. Where Are the Carrots?
Mmm! This Cake Is Delicious!

• Asking for and Reporting Information • Want–Desire
• Hesitating • Checking and Indicating Understanding

We're Looking for a Two-Bedroom Apartment Downtown

two-bedroom downtown

A. We're looking for a two-bedroom apartment downtown.

B. I think I have an apartment for you.

A. Oh, good. Can you describe it?

B. Yes. It has two bedrooms, a large living room, and a very nice kitchen.

1. three-bedroom near the hospital

2. one-bedroom near the park

3. two-bedroom near the university

4. one-bedroom uptown

5. two-bedroom near the beach

"WE'RE LOOKING FOR A TWO-BEDROOM APARTMENT DOWNTOWN"

Now present your own conversations.

Is There a Refrigerator in the Kitchen?

a refrigerator – kitchen?

windows – living room?

4

A. Is there a refrigerator in the kitchen?

B. Yes, there is. There's a very nice refrigerator in the kitchen.

A. And how many windows are there in the living room?

B. Hmm. Let me see. I think there are four windows in the living room.

a shower – bathroom?

cabinets – kitchen?

6

1.

a fireplace – living room?

closets – bedroom?

2

2.

a stove – kitchen?

floors – building?

8

3.

a closet – bedroom?

elevators – building?

3

4.

a dishwasher – kitchen?

parking spaces – parking lot?

9 or 10

5.

"IS THERE A REFRIGERATOR IN THE KITCHEN?"

Now present your own conversations.

How Much Is the Rent?

A. How much is the rent?

B. It's $700 a month.

A. Does that include utilities?

B. It includes everything except electricity.

A. Hmm. $700 a month plus electricity?

B. That's right.   Do you want to see the apartment?

A. Yes, I think so.

$900 — gas

1.

$400 — heat

2.

$650 — electricity

3.

$575 — gas

4.

$725 — the parking fee

5.

Now present your own conversations.

Where Do You Want This Sofa?

A. Where do you want this sofa?

B. That sofa? Hmm. Put it in the living room.

A. And how about these chairs?

B. Those chairs? Let me see. Please put them in the dining room.

1.

2.

3.

4.

5.

"WHERE DO YOU WANT THIS SOFA?"

Now present your own conversations.

There Aren't Any More Cookies

A. What are you looking for?

B. A cookie.

A. I'm afraid there aren't any more cookies.

B. There aren't?

A. No. I'll get some more when I go to the supermarket.

1. *a tomato*

2. *an apple*

3. *a banana*

4. *an egg*

5. *an orange*

"THERE AREN'T ANY MORE COOKIES"

Now present your own conversations.

There Isn't Any More Milk

A. What are you looking for?

B. Milk.

A. I'm afraid there isn't any more milk.

B. There isn't?

A. No. I'll get some more when I go to the supermarket.

1.

2.

3.

4.

5.

Now present your own conversations.

Excuse Me. Where Are the Carrots?

A. Excuse me. Where are the carrots?

B. They're in Aisle J.

A. I'm sorry. Did you say "A"?

B. No. "J."

A. Oh. Thank you.

A. Excuse me. Where's the butter?

B. It's in Aisle 3.

A. I'm sorry. Did you say "C"?

B. No. "3."

A. Oh. Thanks.

1.

2.

3.

4.

5.

Now present your own conversations.

INTERCHANGE
Mmm! This Cake Is Delicious!

A. Mmm! This cake is delicious!

B. I'm glad you like it.

A. What's in it?

B. Let me think . . . some eggs, some sugar, some flour, and some raisins.

A. Well, it's excellent!

B. Thank you for saying so.

A. Mmm! These egg rolls are delicious!

B. I'm glad you like them.

A. What's in them?

B. Let me see . . . some cabbage, some pork, some shrimp, and some bean sprouts.

A. Well, they're excellent!

B. Thank you for saying so.

You're eating at your friend's home. The food is delicious. Compliment your friend, using the model dialogs above as a guide. Feel free to adapt and expand the models any way you wish.

Topic Vocabulary

Housing

balcony
bathroom
bedroom
dining room
kitchen
living room
patio

cabinet
closet
dishwasher
fireplace
refrigerator
shower
stove
window

apartment
building

elevator
floor
parking lot
parking space

electricity
gas
heat
parking fee
rent
utilities

Furniture

bed
chair
crib
lamp
picture
plant
rug

sofa
table
TV
waterbed

Foods

apple
banana
bean sprouts
bread
butter
cabbage
cake
carrot
cheese
coffee
cookie
egg
egg rolls
flour

ice cream
lettuce
milk
orange
peach
pork
potato
raisins
rice
shrimp
sugar
tomato
yogurt

Community

beach
hospital
park
supermarket
university

Grammar

Singular/Plural

It has one bedroom.
It has two bedrooms.

There's a nice refrigerator.
There are four windows.

That sofa? Put **it** in the living room.
Those chairs? Put **them** in the dining room.

Where are the   carrots?   /s/
potatoes?   /z/
peaches?   /ɪz/

Count/Non-Count Nouns

Count

There aren't any more   cookies.
tomatoes.
apples.

Where are the   carrots?
potatoes?
peaches?

These egg rolls are delicious!

Non-Count

There isn't any more   milk.
bread.
cheese.

Where's the   butter?
sugar?
rice?

This cake is delicious.

This/That/These/Those

Where do you want **this** sofa?
That sofa?
How about **these** chairs?
Those chairs?

There Is/There Are

Is there a refrigerator?
Yes, **there is. There's** a refrigerator in the kitchen.

How many windows **are there**?
There are four windows.

There isn't any more milk.
There aren't any more cookies.

Articles: A/An

A cookie.   An apple.
A tomato.   An egg.
A banana.   An orange.

Article: The

Where are **the** carrots?
Where's **the** butter?

Some/Any

I'll get **some** more.
There aren't **any** more cookies.

Imperatives

Put it in the living room.
Please put them in the dining room.

Have/Has

I **have** an apartment for you.
It **has** two bedrooms.

Simple Present Tense vs. To Be

How much **is** the rent?

Do you want to see the apartment?
Does that include utilities?

Cardinal Numbers: 100–999

100   one hundred
200   two hundred
300   three hundred
·   ·
·   ·
900   nine hundred
999   nine hundred (and) ninety-nine

Functions and Conversation Strategies in this chapter are listed in the Appendix, page 194.

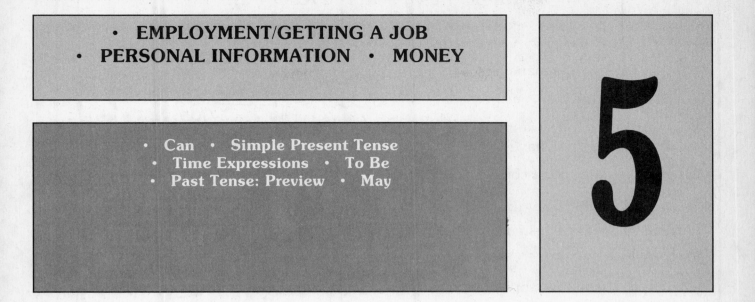

EMPLOYMENT/GETTING A JOB
PERSONAL INFORMATION · MONEY

- Can · Simple Present Tense
- Time Expressions · To Be
- Past Tense: Preview · May

5

What Job Do You Have Open?
Can I Come In for an Interview?
I'm a Very Experienced Sales Clerk
I'm Sure I Can Learn Quickly
Are You Currently Employed?
Can You Tell Me a Little More About the Position?
Can You Tell Me About the Work Schedule
and the Salary?
Tell Me a Little More About Yourself

- Asking for and Reporting Information
- Asking for and Reporting Additional Information
- Ability/Inability · Certainty/Uncertainty
- Checking and Indicating Understanding · Hesitating

What Job Do You Have Open?

A. Can I talk to the manager?

B. Yes. I'm the manager.

A. I saw your "help wanted" sign. What job do you have open?

B. We're looking for a cook.

A. I'd like to apply.

B. Can you make eggs and sandwiches?

A. Yes, I can.

B. Okay. Here's an application form.

A. Thank you.

cook

make eggs and sandwiches?

mechanic

1. fix cars?

housekeeper

2. clean rooms and make beds?

cashier

3. use a cash register?

dishwasher

4. operate kitchen equipment?

stock clerk

5. lift heavy boxes?

"WHAT JOB DO YOU HAVE OPEN?"

Now present your own conversations.

Can I Come In for an Interview?

Ann Kramer

A. I'm calling about your ad for a secretary. Is that job still open?

B. Yes, it is. Can you type?

A. Yes, I can. Can I come in for an interview?

B. Yes. What's your name?

A. Ann Kramer.

B. Can you come in on Monday at 10:00?*

A. On Monday at 10:00? Yes. Thanks very much.

Peter Grant

drive a truck?

1. Tuesday
2:00

Gary Johnson

operate office equipment?

2. Wednesday
3:00

Brenda Hall

use laboratory equipment?

3. Thursday
1:30†

Norman Taylor

teach Biology and Chemistry?

4. Friday
9:30

Maria Lopez

use a computer?

5. Monday
11:30

"CAN I COME IN FOR AN INTERVIEW?"

Now present your own conversations.

* 10:00 = ten o'clock   † 1:30 = one thirty

I'm a Very Experienced Sales Clerk

A. I'm a very experienced sales clerk.

B. Tell me about your skills.

A. I know how to talk with customers and I can use a cash register.

B. I see. And do you know how to take inventory?

A. Yes, I do. I can take inventory very well.

1. secretary

2. medical technician

3. actor

4. custodian

5. chef

Now present your own conversations.

I'm Sure I Can Learn Quickly

use a copying machine?

A. Can you use a copying machine?

B. No, I can't. But I'm sure I can learn quickly.

A. Hmm. We really need somebody who can use a copying machine.

B. I understand. I know I can learn very quickly.

A. Are you sure?

B. Yes. I'm positive.

make salads?

1.

operate a forklift?

2.

repair vacuum cleaners and toasters?

3.

use word-processing equipment?

4.

play rock 'n roll?

5.

"I'M SURE I CAN LEARN QUICKLY"

Now present your own conversations.

Are You Currently Employed?

salesperson

yes
Tyler's Department Store
3 years

waiter

no
the Seven Seas Restaurant
1 year

A. Are you currently employed?

B. Yes, I am. I work at Tyler's Department Store.

A. And what is your position there?

B. I'm a salesperson.

A. How long have you worked there?

B. Three years.

A. Are you currently employed?

B. No, not at the moment. My last job was at the Seven Seas Restaurant.

A. And what was your position there?

B. I was a waiter.

A. How long did you work there?

B. One year.

typist

waitress

ESL* teacher

1. yes
the Crown Insurance
Company
2 years

2. no
the Broadway Coffee
Shop
9 months

3. no
the Adult Learning
Center
5 years

security guard

clown

"ARE YOU CURRENTLY EMPLOYED?"

4. yes
the Ajax Security
Company
7 months

5. no
the Rinkydink Brothers
Circus
30 years

Now present your own
conversations.

* ESL = English as a Second Language

44

Can You Tell Me a Little More About the Position?

A. Can you tell me a little more about the position?

B. Certainly. What do you want to know?

A. What are the job responsibilities of a stock clerk here?

B. A stock clerk stocks the shelves and cleans the aisles. Do you think you can do that?

A. Yes, definitely! I stock the shelves and clean the aisles in my present job.

1. a housekeeper

2. a waiter

3. a salesperson

4. a medical technician

5. a security guard

Now present your own conversations.

* I.D. = identification

Can You Tell Me About the Work Schedule and the Salary?

A. Can you tell me about the work schedule?

B. Yes. Hours are from nine (9:00)* to five thirty (5:30), with a lunch break at one (1:00).*

A. I see. And may I ask about the salary?

B. Yes. The salary is five dollars ($5.00) an hour. Do you have any other questions?

A. No. I don't think so.

8:30 – 5:00
12:30
six dollars ($6.00) an hour

1.

8:00 – 4:30
12 noon
two hundred and fifty dollars ($250) a week

2.

7:30 – 6:00
11:30
fifty dollars ($50) a day

3.

7:00 – 3:30
11:00
fifteen thousand dollars ($15,000) a year

4.

9:00 – 5:00
noon
eighteen thousand dollars ($18,000) a year

5.

"CAN YOU TELL ME ABOUT THE WORK SCHEDULE AND THE SALARY?"

Now present your own conversations.

* 9:00 = "nine o'clock" or "nine"
  1:00 = "one o'clock" or "one"

46

INTERCHANGE
Tell Me a Little More About Yourself

A. Before we finish, tell me a little more about yourself.

B. All right. Let's see . . . I'm married. My husband's name is Richard. He's a security guard at the National Motors factory. We have two children, a son and a daughter.

A. And where are you originally from?

B. I'm from Dallas.

A. Do you have any hobbies or special interests?

B. Yes. I play the piano and I take dance lessons.

A. I see. Tell me, do YOU have any questions for ME?

B. No, I don't think so. I appreciate the time you've taken to talk with me.

A. My pleasure. You'll hear from us soon.

B. Thank you very much.

A. Before we finish, tell me a little more about yourself.

B. All right. Let's see . . . _____.

A. And where are you originally from?

B. I'm from _____.

A. Do you have any hobbies or special interests?

B. Yes. I _____.

A. I see. Tell me, do YOU have any questions for ME?

B. No, I don't think so. I appreciate the time you've taken to talk with me.

A. My pleasure. You'll hear from us soon.

B. Thank you very much.

You're at a job interview. Create an original conversation using the model dialog above as a guide. Feel free to adapt and expand the model any way you wish.

CHAPTER 5 SUMMARY

Topic Vocabulary

Occupations

actor
cashier
chef
clown
cook
custodian
data processor
dishwasher
driver
ESL teacher
housekeeper
lab technician
manager
mechanic
medical technician
office assistant
sales clerk
salesperson
science teacher
secretary
security guard
stock clerk
typist
waiter
waitress

Job Skills

act
bake
check *I.D. cards*
clean *rooms*
clean *the aisles*
cook *American food*
dance
do *lab tests*
drive *a truck*
file
fix *cars*
guard *the building entrance*
help *customers*
lift *heavy boxes*
make *beds*
make *eggs and sandwiches*
make *salads*
operate *a forklift*
operate *a heating system*
operate *kitchen equipment*
operate *office equipment*
operate *X-ray equipment*
play *rock 'n roll*
prepare *international food*
repair *things*
repair *vacuum cleaners and toasters*
serve *the food*

sing
stock *the shelves*
take *blood*
take *inventory*
take *orders*
take *shorthand*
talk *with customers*
teach *Biology*
type
use *a cash register*
use *a computer*
use *a copying machine*
use *cleaning equipment*
use *laboratory equipment*
use *word-processing equipment*

Family Members

children
daughter
husband
son

Getting a Job

ad
application form
employed
experienced

"help wanted" sign
hobbies
hours
interview
job
job responsibilities
lunch break
position
salary
skills
special interests
work schedule

Days of the Week

Sunday
Monday
Tuesday
Wednesday
Thursday
Friday
Saturday

Time

hour
day
week
month
year

Grammar

Can

Can you make eggs and sandwiches?
Yes, I **can.**
No, I **can't.**

I **can** use a cash register.
We really need somebody who
   can use a copying machine.

Can I talk to the manager?
Can you tell me a little more
   about the position?

Simple Present Tense

/s/
   I stock the shelves.
A stock clerk stock**s** the shelves

/z/
   I clean rooms.
A housekeeper clean**s** rooms.

/ɪz/
   I use a cash register.
A salesperson use**s** a cash register.

Do you have any hobbies?

May

May I ask about the salary?

Time Expressions

1:00 one o'clock (one)
2:00 two o'clock (two)
3:00 three o'clock (three)
 •   •
 •   •
12:00 twelve o'clock (twelve)

1:30 one thirty
2:30 two thirty
3:30 three thirty
 •   •
 •   •
12:30 twelve thirty

On Monday **at** 10:00.

Hours are **from** 9:00 **to** 5:30.

The salary is $5.00 **an hour.**
                $250   **a week.**
                $50   **a day.**
                $15,000 **a year.**

To Be

Are you currently employed?
   Yes, I **am.**
What **is** your position there?
   I'm a salesperson.

am **I'm** married.
is My husband's name **is**
        Richard.
        He's a security guard.
are Where **are** you originally
        from?

Past Tense: Preview

My last job **was** at the Seven
Seas Restaurant.

What **was** your position there?
   I **was** a waiter.

How long **did** you work there?
   One year.

Cardinal Numbers: 1,000–1,000,000

1,000 one thousand
2,000 two thousand
3,000 three thousand
 •   •
 •   •
10,000 ten thousand
100,000 one hundred thousand
1,000,000 one million

Functions and Conversation Strategies in this chapter are listed in the Appendix, page 195.

• HEALTH • DRUG STORE • EMERGENCIES

• Imperatives • Have • Can • Should
• Simple Present Tense vs. To Be
• Present Continuous Tense • Short Answers
• Time Expressions • Possessive Nouns
• Prepositions of Location • Count/Non-Count Nouns

I Have a Headache
What Do You Recommend?
Do You Want to Make an Appointment?
Do You Smoke?
Touch Your Toes
You Should Go on a Diet
Take One Tablet Three Times a Day
I Want to Report an Emergency!

• Asking for and Reporting Information • Instructing
• Advice—Suggestions • Directions—Location
• Checking and Indicating Understanding
• Initiating a Topic

I Have a Headache

A. You know . . . you don't look very well. Are you feeling okay?

B. No, not really.

A. What's the matter?

B. I have a headache.

A. I'm sorry to hear that.

an earache

1.

a stomachache

2.

a toothache

3.

a sore throat

4.

a backache

5.

"I HAVE A HEADACHE"

Now present your own conversations.

What Do You Recommend?

in Aisle 2 on the right

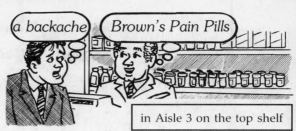

in Aisle 3 on the top shelf

A. Excuse me. Can you help me?

B. Yes.

A. I have a bad cold. What do you recommend?

B. I recommend Maxi-Fed Cold Medicine.

A. Maxi-Fed Cold Medicine?

B. Yes.

A. Where can I find it?

B. It's in Aisle 2 on the right.

A. Thanks.

A. Excuse me. Can you help me?

B. Yes.

A. I have a backache. What do you recommend?

B. I recommend Brown's Pain Pills.

A. Brown's Pain Pills?

B. Yes.

A. Where can I find them?

B. They're in Aisle 3 on the top shelf.

A. Thank you.

1. in Aisle 1 on the left

2. in Aisle 4 on the bottom shelf

3. in Aisle 2 on the middle shelf

4. in the back near the aspirin

5. in the front near the cash register

Now present your own conversations.

51

Do You Want to Make an Appointment?

John Stevens isn't feeling very well.

A. Doctor's Office.

B. Hello. This is John Stevens. I'm not feeling very well.

A. What's the problem?

B. My right foot hurts very badly.

A. I see. Do you want to make an appointment?

B. Yes, please.

A. Can you come in tomorrow morning at 9:15?*

B. Tomorrow morning at 9:15? Yes. That's fine. Thank you.

1. Karen Fuller isn't feeling very well.

2. Sally Wilson's son isn't feeling very well.

3. Mr. Beck's daughter isn't feeling very well.

4. Ms. Wong isn't feeling very well.

5. Charlie Green's parrot, Willy, isn't feeling very well.

"DO YOU WANT TO MAKE AN APPOINTMENT?"

Now present your own conversations.

* 9:15 = nine fifteen
† 11:45 = eleven forty-five

Do You Smoke?

A. I have just one more question.

B. All right.

A. Do you smoke?

B. No, I don't.

A. Okay. I think that's all the information I need for your medical history. The doctor will see you shortly.

B. Thank you.

1.

2.

3.

4.

5.

Now present your own conversations.

Touch Your Toes

*Touch **your toes.***

A. Touch your toes.
B. My toes?
A. Yes.

*Take off **your shirt.***

A. Take off your shirt.
B. My shirt?
A. Yes.

*Sit **on the table.***

A. Sit on the table.
B. On the table?
A. Yes.

*Hold **your breath.***

A. Hold your breath.
B. Hold my breath?
A. Yes.

*Lie **on your back.***

1.

*Look **at the ceiling.***

2.

Cough.

"UNCLE SAM WANTS YOU!"

3.

*Roll up **your sleeve.***

4.

Say "a-a-h"!

A-A-H

5.

"TOUCH YOUR TOES"

Now present your own conversations.

54

You Should Go on a Diet

weight
go on a diet
lose 15 pounds

A. I'm concerned about your weight.

B. My weight?

A. Yes.   You should go on a diet.

B. I see.

A. I suggest that you lose 15 pounds.

B. I understand.   Thank you for the advice.

1. lungs
stop smoking
quit immediately

2. back
exercise daily
do sit-ups

3. blood pressure
change your diet
stop eating salty and
fatty foods

4. gums
use dental floss
use it daily

5. life style
slow down
take a vacation

"YOU SHOULD GO ON A DIET"

Now present your own
conversations.

Take One Tablet Three Times a Day

1 tablet 3 times a day

A. Here's your medicine.

B. Thank you.

A. Be sure to follow the directions on the label. Take one tablet three times a day.

B. I understand. One tablet three times a day.

A. That's right.

1 pill 4 times a day

1.

2 tablets before each meal

2.

1 teaspoon twice a day

3.

2 capsules after each meal

4.

1 teaspoon 3 times a day

5.

"TAKE ONE TABLET THREE TIMES A DAY"

Now present your own conversations.

INTERCHANGE
I Want to Report an Emergency!

A. Police.

B. I want to report an emergency!

A. Yes?

B. I think my father is having a heart attack!

A. What's your name?

B. Diane Perkins.

A. And the address?

B. 76 Lake Street.

A. Telephone number?

B. 293-7637.

A. All right. We'll be there right away.

B. Thank you.

Diane Perkins
76 Lake Street
293-7637

1. Neal Stockman
193 Davis Avenue
458-9313

2. Janet Brown
17 Park Road
963-2475

3. Carol Weaver
1440 Lexington Boulevard
354-6260

4. Henry Stewart
5 Linden Lane
723-0980

You're reporting an emergency. Create an original conversation using the model dialog above as a guide. Feel free to adapt and expand the model any way you wish.

CHAPTER 6 SUMMARY

Topic Vocabulary

Health

allergies
backache
bleeding
choking
cold
cough
dizzy
earache
headache
heart attack
heart disease
sore throat
stiff neck
stomachache
toothache

back
ear
foot
gums
lungs
neck
toes

blood pressure
diet
life style
weight

Personal Information

name
address
telephone number

Medicine

aspirin
cold medicine
cough syrup
ear drops
medication
pain pills
penicillin
throat lozenges

capsule
pill
tablet
teaspoon

Emergencies

ambulance
emergency
fire department
hospital
police
police emergency unit

Family Members

daughter
father
son
wife

Grammar

Imperatives

Touch your toes.
Be sure to follow the directions on the label.

Have

I **have** a headache.

Can

Can you help me?

Should

You **should** go on a diet.

Simple Present Tense vs. To Be

Do you smoke?
  No, I **don't**.

Are you allergic to penicillin?
  No, **I'm not**.
Is there a history of heart disease in your family?
  No, there **isn't**.

Present Continuous Tense

I'm not **feeling** very well.
He's feeling very dizzy.
My ears **are** **ringing**.

Short Answers

No, I don't.
No, I'm not.

No, there isn't.

Time Expressions

1:15	one fifteen
2:15	two fifteen
3:15	three fifteen
•	•
•	•
12:15	twelve fifteen
1:45	one forty-five
2:45	two forty-five
3:45	three forty-five
•	•
•	•
12:45	twelve forty-five

this morning
this afternoon
tomorrow morning
tomorrow afternoon
this Friday
next Monday

tomorrow morning **at** 9:15

Take one tablet three **times a day.**
                         twice a day.
                         before each meal.
                         after each meal.

Possessive Nouns

Doctor**'s** Office.
Sally Wilson**'s** son isn't feeling very well.

Prepositions of Location

It's **in** Aisle 2 **on** the right.
It's **in** Aisle 2 **near** the aspirin.

Count/Non-Count Nouns

Count

I recommend Brown's Pain Pill**s**.
  Where can I find **them**?
They're in Aisle 3.

Non-Count

I recommend Maxi-Fed Cold Medicine.
  Where can I find **it**?
It's in Aisle 2.

Functions and Conversation Strategies in this chapter are listed in the Appendix, pages 195–196.

Who do you think these people are?
What do you think they're talking about?
Create conversations based on these scenes and act them out.

1.

2.

3.

4.

5.

6.

7.

8.

- **CLOTHING** • **DEPARTMENT STORE**
- **MONEY** • **POST OFFICE**

- Singular/Plural • Prepositions of Location
- Adjectives • Too + Adjective
- Ordinal Numbers • Want to
- Question Formation

I'm Looking for a Shirt
May I Help You?
It's Too Short
Excuse Me. Where Are the Rest Rooms?
I'd Like to Buy This Watch
I Want to Return This Fan
I Want to Buy Some Stamps, Please
I'd Like to Mail This Package

- Want–Desire • Directions–Location
- Satisfaction/Dissatisfaction
- Attracting Attention • Gratitude
- Checking and Indicating Understanding
- Hesitating

I'm Looking for a Shirt

a shirt — in Aisle 3

A. Excuse me. Can you help me?
B. Certainly.
A. I'm looking for a shirt.
B. Shirts are in Aisle 3.
A. Thank you.

a tie — on that counter

A. Excuse me. Can you help me?
B. Certainly.
A. I'm looking for a tie.
B. Ties are on that counter.
A. Thank you.

a dress — over there

A. Excuse me. Can you help me?
B. Certainly.
A. I'm looking for a dress.
B. Dresses are over there.
A. Thank you.

a pair of pants — on that rack

A. Excuse me. Can you help me?
B. Certainly.
A. I'm looking for a pair of pants.
B. Pants are on that rack.
A. Thank you.

1. a coat — on that rack

2. an umbrella — on that counter

3. a blouse — over there on that table

4. a pair of shoes — in the front of the store

5. a hat — in the back of the store

"I'M LOOKING FOR A SHIRT"

Now present your own conversations.

62

May I Help You?

A. May I help you?

B. Yes, please. I'm looking for a belt.

A. What size do you want?

B. Size 36.

A. And what color?

B. Black.

A. Okay. Let's see . . . a size 36 black belt. Here you are.

B. Thank you very much.

1.

2.

3.

4.

5.

Now present your own conversations.

* 15½ = fifteen and a half

It's Too Short

short

jacket

long

pants

A. How does the jacket fit?

B. It's too short.

A. Do you want to try on another one?

B. Yes, please.

A. Okay. Here. I think this jacket will fit better.

B. Thanks very much.

A. How do the pants fit?

B. They're too long.

A. Do you want to try on another pair?

B. Yes, please.

A. Okay. Here. I think these pants will fit better.

B. Thanks very much.

big

1. skirt

tight

2. sneakers

small

3. blouse

large

4. gloves

tight

5. suit

"IT'S TOO SHORT"

Now present your own conversations.

Excuse Me. Where Are the Rest Rooms?

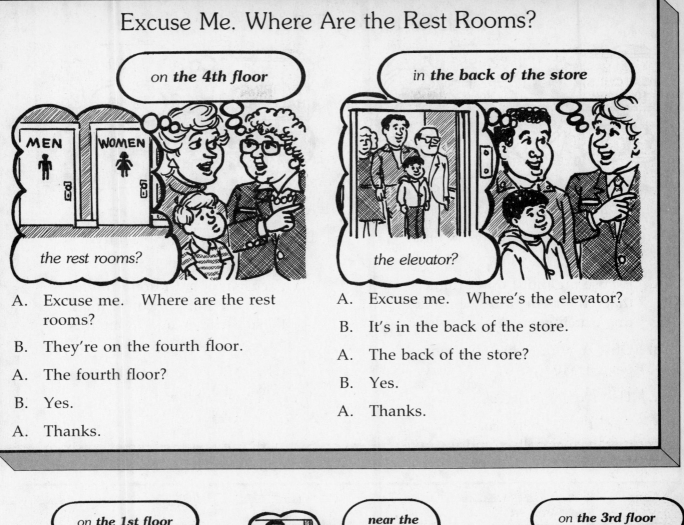

on the 4th floor

the rest rooms?

A. Excuse me. Where are the rest rooms?
B. They're on the fourth floor.
A. The fourth floor?
B. Yes.
A. Thanks.

in the back of the store

the elevator?

A. Excuse me. Where's the elevator?
B. It's in the back of the store.
A. The back of the store?
B. Yes.
A. Thanks.

on the 1st floor

refrigerators?

1.

near the elevator

the dressing room?

2.

on the 3rd floor

TVs and radios?

3.

on the 2nd floor

bedroom furniture?

4.

in the basement

the Customer Service Counter?

5.

"EXCUSE ME. WHERE ARE THE REST ROOMS?"

Now present your own conversations.

I'd Like to Buy This Watch

A. I'd like to buy this watch.

B. Okay. That's twenty-six ninety-five ($26.95).

A. Excuse me, but I don't think that's the right price. I think this watch is on sale this week.

B. Oh. You're right. It's ten percent (10%) off. I'm sorry.

A. That's okay.

B. With the tax, that comes to twenty-five dollars and forty-seven cents ($25.47).

A. I'd like to buy these earrings.

B. Okay. That's twelve fifty ($12.50).

A. Excuse me, but I don't think that's the right price. I think these earrings are on sale this week.

B. Oh. You're right. They're half price. I apologize.

A. That's okay.

B. With the tax, that comes to six dollars and fifty-six cents ($6.56).

1. necklace

2. boots

3. camera

4. stockings

5. typewriter

"I'D LIKE TO BUY THIS WATCH"

Now present your own conversations.

I Want to Return This Fan

fan
noisy

A. I want to return this fan.

B. What's the matter with it?

A. It's too noisy.

B. Do you want to exchange it?

A. No.   I'd like a refund, please.

B. Okay.   Do you have the receipt?

A. Yes.   Here you are.

jeans
short

A. I want to return these jeans.

B. What's the matter with them?

A. They're too short.

B. Do you want to exchange them?

A. No.   I'd like a refund, please.

B. Okay.   Do you have the receipt?

A. Yes.   Here you are.

1. purse
small

2. pajamas
tight

3. coat
heavy

4. videogames
easy

5. textbook
difficult

Now present your own
conversations.

I Want to Buy Some Stamps, Please

A. I want to buy some stamps, please.

B. I'm sorry. You're at the wrong window. You can buy stamps at Window Number 2.

A. Window Number 2?

B. Yes.

A. Thank you.

1. mail a package

2. buy a money order

3. send a registered letter

4. buy an aerogramme

5. file a change of address form

Now present your own conversations.

INTERCHANGE
I'd Like to Mail This Package

A. I'd like to mail this package.

B. Where's it going?

A. To Detroit.

B. How do you want to send it?

A. First class, please.

B. Do you want to insure it?

A. Hmm. I don't know.

B. Well, is it valuable?

A. Yes, it is. It's a camera I'm sending to my brother. Please insure it for fifty dollars ($50).

B. All right. That's four dollars and thirty-seven cents ($4.37), please.

A. I'd like to mail this package.

B. Where's it going?

A. To _____.

B. How do you want to send it?

A. First class, please.

B. Do you want to insure it?

A. Hmm. I don't know.

B. Well, is it valuable?

A. Yes, it is. It's a _____ I'm sending to _____. Please insure it for _____ dollars.

B. All right. That's _____ dollars and _____ cents, please.

You're mailing a package at the post office. Create an original conversation using the model dialog above as a guide. Feel free to adapt and expand the model any way you wish.

Topic Vocabulary

Clothing

belt
blouse
coat
dress
hat
jacket
necklace
purse
raincoat
shirt
skirt
suit
sweater
tie
umbrella
watch

boots
earrings
gloves
jeans
pajamas
pants
shoes
sneakers
socks
stockings

Department Store

aisle
basement
counter
Customer Service Counter
dressing room
elevator
price
rack
receipt
refund
rest rooms
sale
table
tax

bedroom furniture
camera
fan
radio
refrigerator
textbook
TV
typewriter
videogame

Colors

black
blue
brown
gray
green
red
white
yellow

Describing

big
difficult
easy
heavy
large
long
noisy
short
small
tight

Post Office

aerogramme
change of address form
money order
package
registered letter
stamps

first class
insure
window

Grammar

Singular/Plural

/s/
I'm looking for **a shirt.**
Shirts are in Aisle 3.

/z/
I'm looking for **a tie.**
Ties are in Aisle 3.

/ɪz/
I'm looking for **a dress.**
Dresses are in Aisle 3.

I'm looking for **a pair of** pants.
　　　　　　　 a pair of shoes.

I'd like to buy **this** watch.
I'd like to buy **these** earrings.

How does the　　　How do the pants
　jacket fit?　　　　fit?
What's the matter　What the matter
　with **it**?　　　　with **them**?
It's too long.　　**They're** too long.
Do you want to　　Do you want to
　try on **another**　try on **another**
　one?　　　　　**pair**?

Where's the elevator?
Where **are** the rest rooms?

Prepositions of Location

Shirts are **in** Aisle 3.
　　　　　on that counter.
　　　　　in the back of the
　　　　　store.
　　　　　in the front of the
　　　　　store.
　　　　　near the elevator.
　　　　　over there.

Adjectives

A **size 36 black** belt.
A **medium green** sweater.
A **small brown** raincoat.

It's too **short.**

Too + Adjective

It's **too short.**
They're **too long.**

Ordinal Numbers

1st　first
2nd　second
3rd　third
4th　fourth

Want To

I **want to** return this fan.

Do you **want to** insure it?
How do you **want to** send it?

Question Formation

Is it valuable?
Where's it going?

Do you want to insure it?
How do you want to send it?

Functions and Conversation Strategies in this chapter are listed in the Appendix, pages 196–197.

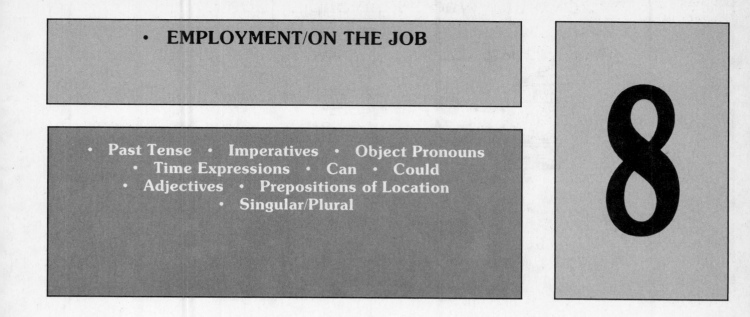

· EMPLOYMENT/ON THE JOB

8

- Past Tense · Imperatives · Object Pronouns
- Time Expressions · Can · Could
- Adjectives · Prepositions of Location
- Singular/Plural

Excuse Me. Where's the Supply Room?
Please Take This Box to Mr. Miller on the 3rd Floor
Can You Show Me How to Turn On This Machine?
Could You Tell Me How to Transfer a Call?
Could You Possibly Show Me How?
Did I Wash the Glasses All Right?
Did I Type the Letters All Right?
You're Required to Wear Your Helmet at All Times
I'm Free Now. What Do You Want Me to Do?

- Requests · Instructing · Attracting Attention
- Approval/Disapproval · Apologizing
- Checking and Indicating Understanding
- Asking for Repetition · Hesitating
- Focusing Attention

Excuse Me. Where's the Supply Room?

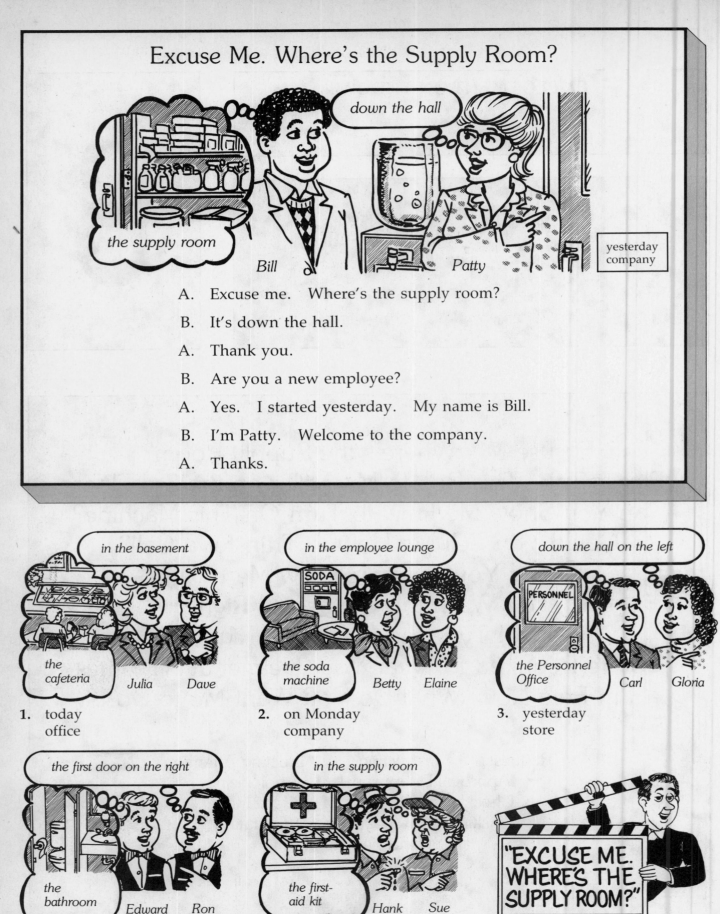

A. Excuse me. Where's the supply room?

B. It's down the hall.

A. Thank you.

B. Are you a new employee?

A. Yes. I started yesterday. My name is Bill.

B. I'm Patty. Welcome to the company.

A. Thanks.

1. today
office

2. on Monday
company

3. yesterday
store

4. this morning
restaurant

5. last week
factory

"EXCUSE ME. WHERE'S THE SUPPLY ROOM?"

Now present your own conversations.

Please Take This Box to Mr. Miller on the 3rd Floor

A. Please take this box to Mr. Miller on the 3rd floor.

B. To Mr. Miller?

A. Yes.

B. I'm sorry, but I'm new here. What does he look like?

A. He's tall, with brown hair.

B. Okay. I'll do it right away.

Please take this box **to Mr. Miller** on the 3rd floor.

He's tall, with brown hair.

height	weight	hair	
very tall	very thin	curly	brown
tall	thin	straight	black
average height	heavy		blond/blonde
short	very heavy	dark	red
very short		light	gray

Please give this letter **to Mrs. Hill** in the Personnel Office.

1. She's short, with blonde hair.

Please take this package **to Mr. Newton** in Shipping.

2. He's very tall and thin.

Please get some clean glasses **from Fred** in the kitchen.

3. He's heavy, with curly dark hair.

Please give these keys **to Ms. Johnson** at the front desk.

4. She's average height, with gray hair.

Please get some typing paper **from Miss Walters** in Word Processing.

5. She's tall and thin, with straight black hair.

"PLEASE TAKE THIS BOX TO MR. MILLER ON THE 3RD FLOOR"

Now present your own conversations.

Can You Show Me How to Turn On This Machine?

Press this button.

turn on this machine

A. Excuse me. Can you help me for a minute?

B. Sure. What is it?

A. Can you show me how to turn on this machine?

B. Yes. Press this button.

A. I see. Thanks very much.

B. You're welcome.

Pull this chain.

1. turn off this light

Push this button.

2. open this door

Flip this switch.

3. start this dishwasher

Put in your time card like this.

4. punch in

Pull the lever like this.

5. stop the conveyor belt

"CAN YOU SHOW ME HOW TO TURN ON THIS MACHINE?"

Now present your own conversations.

Could You Tell Me How to Transfer a Call?

A. Excuse me. Could you help me for a minute?

B. Certainly. What is it?

A. Could you tell me how to transfer a call?

B. Sure. Press the red button. Then, dial the other office and hang up.

A. I see. First, I press the red button. Then, I dial the other office and hang up. Right?

B. Yes. That's right.

A. Thank you.

B. You're welcome.

Press the red button.

Dial the other office and hang up.

transfer a call

Set the amount.

Put the envelope in.

1. use the postage machine

Put a match in the hole at the bottom.

Turn on the gas.

2. light this oven

Pull the handle to close the door.

Push the black button.

3. operate the freight elevator

Put your name and employee number at the top.

List your hours and sign at the bottom.

Name: Ann Wade
#: 923002563
M 9-5
T 9-5
W 9-1
TH 9-7
F 9-5
Signed: Ann Wade

4. fill out this timesheet

Flip the switch to turn it on.

Hold the dish here and lift the handle.

5. use the ice cream machine

"COULD YOU TELL ME HOW TO TRANSFER A CALL?"

Now present your own conversations.

Could You Possibly Show Me How?

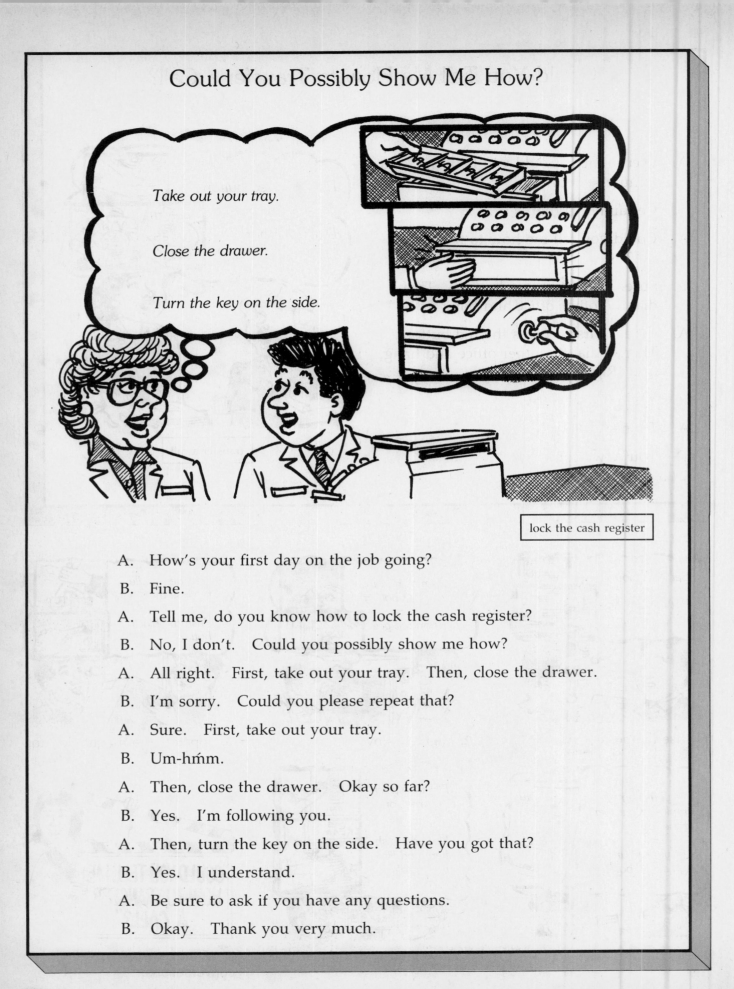

Take out your tray.

Close the drawer.

Turn the key on the side.

lock the cash register

A. How's your first day on the job going?

B. Fine.

A. Tell me, do you know how to lock the cash register?

B. No, I don't.   Could you possibly show me how?

A. All right.   First, take out your tray.   Then, close the drawer.

B. I'm sorry.   Could you please repeat that?

A. Sure.   First, take out your tray.

B. Um-hḿm.

A. Then, close the drawer.   Okay so far?

B. Yes.   I'm following you.

A. Then, turn the key on the side.   Have you got that?

B. Yes.   I understand.

A. Be sure to ask if you have any questions.

B. Okay.   Thank you very much.

A. How's your first day on the job going?

B. Fine.

A. Tell me, do you know how to _____?

B. No, I don't. Could you possibly show me how?

A. All right. First, _____.
Then, _____.

B. I'm sorry. Could you please repeat that?

A. Sure. First, _____.

B. Um-hḿm.

A. Then, _____. Okay so far?

B. Yes. I'm following you.

A. Then, _____. Have you got that?

B. Yes. I understand.

A. Be sure to ask if you have any questions.

B. Okay. Thank you very much.

Place the original on the glass.

Put down the cover.

Press the start button.

1. use the copying machine

Spray the wax on the floor.

Flip this switch to turn on the machine.

Go back and forth like this.

2. use the floor polishing machine

Write the date and the amount on the slip.

Place the slip and the credit card in the machine.

Ask the customer to sign and give the customer the top copy.

3. do a credit card sale

"COULD YOU POSSIBLY SHOW ME HOW?"

Now present your own conversations.

Did I Wash the Glasses All Right?

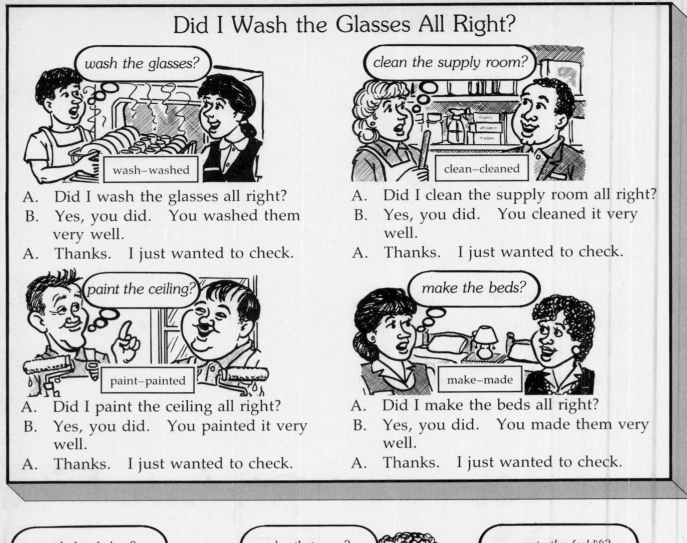

wash the glasses?

wash–washed

A. Did I wash the glasses all right?
B. Yes, you did. You washed them very well.
A. Thanks. I just wanted to check.

clean the supply room?

clean–cleaned

A. Did I clean the supply room all right?
B. Yes, you did. You cleaned it very well.
A. Thanks. I just wanted to check.

paint the ceiling?

paint–painted

A. Did I paint the ceiling all right?
B. Yes, you did. You painted it very well.
A. Thanks. I just wanted to check.

make the beds?

make–made

A. Did I make the beds all right?
B. Yes, you did. You made them very well.
A. Thanks. I just wanted to check.

stock the shelves?

1. stock–stocked

play that song?

2. play–played

operate the forklift?

3. operate–operated

write the reports?

4. write–wrote

give the speech?

5. give–gave

"DID I WASH THE GLASSES ALL RIGHT?"

Now present your own conversations.

Did I Type the Letters All Right?

A. Did I type the letters all right?

B. Actually, you didn't. You typed them rather poorly.

A. Oh? What did I do wrong?

B. You made several spelling mistakes.

A. Oh. I'm sorry.

B. Don't worry about it. You're new on the job.

1. cook–cooked

2. inspect–inspected

3. set–set

4. repair–repaired

5. do–did

Now present your own conversations.

You're Required to Wear Your Helmet at All Times

A. Johnson?

B. Yes, sir?*

A. Where's your helmet?

B. My helmet?   Uh . . . I'm afraid I left† it in my car.

A. You know, you're required to wear your helmet at all times.

B. I'm sorry.   I forgot.†

1.

Karen
gloves — in the bathroom

2.

Peggy
hairnet — in my jacket

3.

Mr. Fuller
lab coat — in the supply room

4.

Miss Horner
safety glasses — in my locker

5.

Donald
uniform — at home

Now present your own conversations.

*   sir (to a man)
    ma'am (to a woman)

†   leave–left
    forget–forgot

80

INTERCHANGE
I'm Free Now. What Do You Want Me to Do?

A. I'm free now. What do you want me to do?

B. Please clean the kitchen shelves.

A. I did that already.

B. You did?

A. Yes. I cleaned them an hour ago.

B. Oh, good. Then please sweep the floor.

A. I did THAT already, too.

B. Really?

A. Yes. I swept* it a little while ago. Is there anything else I can do?

B. Hmm. I can't think of anything at the moment.

A. Do you want me to set the tables for tomorrow?

B. Yes. That's a good idea. You know, you're an excellent new employee.

A. Thank you for saying so. I'm very happy to be here.

A. I'm free now. What do you want me to do?
B. Please _____.
A. I did that already.
B. You did?
A. Yes. I _____ an hour ago.
B. Oh, good.   Then please _____.
A. I did THAT already, too.
B. Really?
A. Yes. I _____ a little while ago.   Is there anything else I can do?
B. Hmm.   I can't think of anything at the moment.
A. Do you want me to _____?
B. Yes.   That's a good idea.   You know, you're an excellent new employee.
A. Thank you for saying so.   I'm very happy to be here.

You're on the job and you're free at the moment.   Create an original conversation using the model dialog above as a guide.   Feel free to adapt and expand the model any way you wish.

* sweep–swept

Topic Vocabulary

Places of Work

company
factory
office
restaurant
store

Places on the Job

basement
bathroom
cafeteria
employee lounge
hall
Personnel Office
Shipping
supply room
Word Processing

Protective Clothing

gloves
hairnet
helmet
lab coat
safety glasses
uniform

Job Procedures

clean *the supply room*
close *the drawer*
cook *the eggs*
dial *the other office*
fill out *this timesheet*
fix *the antenna*
flip *this switch*
hang up
hold *the dish*
inspect *the car*
lift *the handle*
light *this oven*
list *your hours*
lock *the cash register*
make *the beds*
open *this door*
operate *the freight elevator*
paint *the ceiling*
place *the original on the glass*
press *this button*
pull *this chain*
punch in
push *this button*
put *a match in the hole*
put down *the cover*
put in *your time card*
repair *the TV*
set *the amount*

sign *at the bottom*
spray *the wax*
start *this dishwasher*
stock *the shelves*
stop *the conveyor belt*
sweep *the floor*
take out *your tray*
transfer *a call*
turn *the key*
turn off *this light*
turn on *the gas*
type *the letters*
use *the postage machine*
wash *the glasses*
write *the date*

Objects on the Job

cash register
conveyor belt
copying machine
first-aid kit
floor
forklift
freight elevator
key
lever
locker
machine
postage machine

soda machine
time card
timesheet
typing paper

Describing People

height
very tall
tall
average height
short
very short

weight
very thin
thin
heavy
very heavy

hair
curly
straight
light
dark
black
blond/blonde
brown
gray
red

Grammar

Past Tense

/**t**/
You wash**ed** them very well.
/**d**/
You clean**ed** it very well.
/**ɪd**/
You paint**ed** it very well.

Did I wash the glasses all right?
Yes, you **did**.
You **didn't**.

What **did** I do wrong?

make–made
Did I **make** the beds all right?
You **made** them very well.

write–wrote
Did I **write** the reports all right?
You **wrote** them very well.

give–gave
Did I **give** the speech all right?
You **gave** it very well.

set–set
Did I **set** the table all right?
You **set** it rather poorly.

do–did
Did I **do** that customer's hair all
right?
You **did** it rather poorly.

leave–left
I **left** it in my car.

forget–forgot
I **forgot**.

sweep–swept
Please **sweep** the floor.
I **swept** it a little while ago.

Imperatives

Please take this box to Mr.
Miller.

Press this button.

Time Expressions

I started **yesterday.**
today.
on Monday.
this morning.
last week.

Object Pronouns

You cleaned **it** very well.
You washed **them** very well.

Can

Can you help me for a minute?

Could

Could you help me for a
minute?

Adjectives

He's **tall**, with **brown** hair.
He's **heavy**, with **curly dark**
hair.

Prepositions of Location

It's **down** the hall.
It's **in** the basement.
It's **on** the left.

Singular/Plural

Where**'s** your helmet?
Where **are** your gloves?

Functions and Conversation Strategies in this chapter are listed in the Appendix, pages 197–198.

- Past Tense • WH-Questions • Future: Going to
- Want to • Like to • Like to vs. Like
- Can • Have to • Time Expressions

What Do You Want to Do Today?
Let's Do Something Outdoors Today
Do You Want to Get Together Tomorrow?
I'm Afraid I Can't. I Have to Work Late
What Are You Going to Do This Weekend?
How Was Your Weekend?
What Movie Did You See?
What Do You Like to Do in Your Free Time?
Do You Like to Go to Movies?

- Want–Desire • Asking for and Reporting Information
- Invitations • Likes/Dislikes • Intention
- Obligation • Checking and Indicating Understanding

What Do You Want to Do Today?

see a movie

It's raining.

A. What do you want to do today?

B. I don't know. What's the weather like?

A. It's raining. Do you want to see a movie?

B. Sure. That's a good idea.

go skiing

1. It's snowing.

have a picnic

2. It's sunny.

go to a museum

3. It's cloudy.

go swimming

4. It's hot.

stay home and watch TV

5. It's cold.

"WHAT DO YOU WANT TO DO TODAY?"

Now present your own conversations.

Let's Do Something Outdoors Today

play–played

A. Let's do something outdoors today.

B. All right. But I don't want to play tennis. We played tennis last weekend.

A. Okay. What do you want to do?

B. I want to go jogging.

A. All right. That sounds like fun.

1. go–went

2. have–had

3. play–played

4. go–went

5. drive–drove

"LET'S DO SOMETHING OUTDOORS TODAY"

Now present your own conversations.

Do You Want to Get Together Tomorrow?

A. Do you want to get together tomorrow?

B. Sure.   What do you want to do?

A. I don't know.   What's the weather forecast?

B. It's going to be hot.

A. It is?

B. Yes.   I heard it on the radio.

A. Let's go to the beach.

B. Okay.   That sounds like fun.

1. be sunny
I read it in the paper.

2. rain
I saw the forecast on TV.

3. be cold
I heard it on the radio.

4. snow
I heard it on the
7 o'clock news.

5. be cloudy
I called the Weather
Information number.

Now present your own
conversations.

I'm Afraid I Can't. I Have to Work Late

go out for dinner **tonight**?

work late

A. Do you want to go out for dinner tonight?

B. Tonight? I'm afraid I can't. I have to work late.

A. That's too bad.

B. Maybe we can go out for dinner some other time.

go skiing **tomorrow**

go to the dentist

1.

go dancing **tomorrow night**?

baby-sit

2.

see a play **this Saturday night**?

study

3.

go to a concert **this Sunday afternoon**?

visit my aunt and uncle

4.

go for a bike ride **this weekend**?

clean the yard

5.

"I'M AFRAID I CAN'T. I HAVE TO WORK LATE"

Now present your own conversations.

What Are You Going to Do This Weekend?

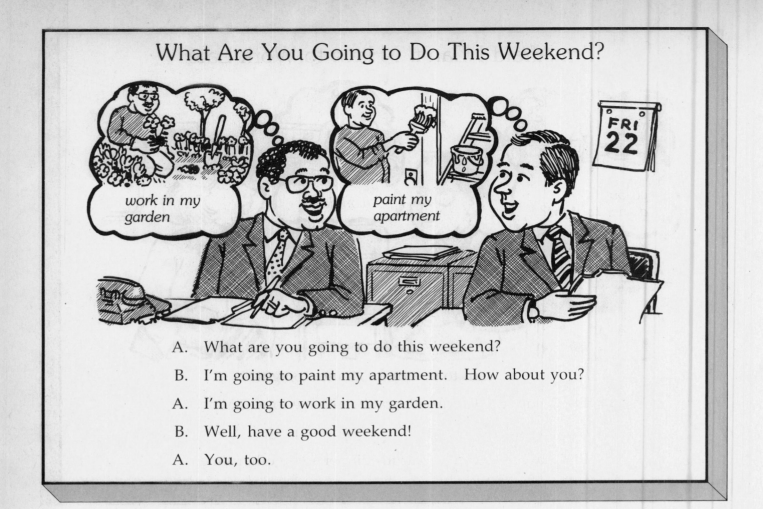

A. What are you going to do this weekend?

B. I'm going to paint my apartment. How about you?

A. I'm going to work in my garden.

B. Well, have a good weekend!

A. You, too.

1.

2.

3.

4.

5.

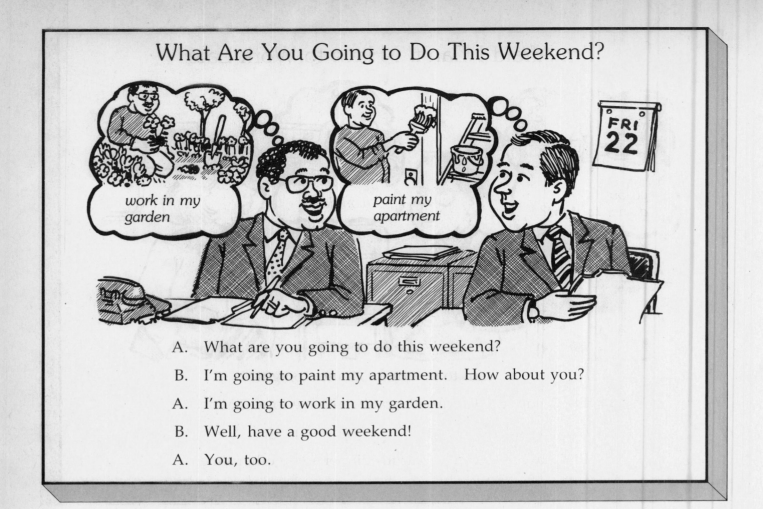

Now present your own conversations.

How Was Your Weekend?

A. Tell me, how was your weekend?

B. It was very nice.

A. What did you do?

B. I went skiing. And how was YOUR weekend?

A. It was okay.

B. Did you do anything special?

A. Not really. I stayed home and watched TV.

1.

2.

3.

4.

5.

Now present your own conversations.

* read–read
take–took

What Movie Did You See?

> What movie did you see?

> "Dancing in the Park"

at the movies

A. I called you yesterday evening, but you weren't home.

B. That's right. I wasn't. I was at the movies.

A. Oh. What movie did you see?

B. I saw "Dancing in the Park."

A. Did you enjoy it?

B. Yes. It was excellent.

> Who did you hear*?

> the Philadelphia Orchestra

1. at the concert hall

> What play did you see?

> "The Friendly Garden"

2. at the theater

> What did you have?

> moussaka

3. at the Greek restaurant

> What game did you see?

> the Yankees against the Red Sox

4. at the baseball stadium

> Who did you go with?

> Millie Hawkins

5. at the county fair

"WHAT MOVIE DID YOU SEE?"

Now present your own conversations.

* hear–heard

What Do You Like to Do in Your Free Time?

Where . . . ?

A. Tell me, what do you like to do in your free time?

B. I like to run.

A. Oh. That's interesting. Where do you like to run?

B. In the park. And how about you? Do YOU like to run?

A. Yes, but I don't like to run in the park. I like to run along the river.

B. Oh. That's interesting.

bread   cakes and cookies

1. What . . .?

at the "Y"*   at the lake

2. Where . . .?

sweaters   baby clothes

3. What . . .?

novels   biographies

4. What kind of books . . .?

people   trees

5. What . . .?

Now present your own conversations.

* "Y" = YMCA or YWCA

INTERCHANGE
Do You Like to Go to Movies?

Do you like to go to movies?
What kind of movies* . . .?
movie star (actor/actress)

* comedies
  westerns
  dramas
  mysteries
  adventure movies
  science fiction movies
  •
  •
  •

A. Tell me, do you like to go to movies?

B. Yes. I like to go to movies a lot.

A. What kind of movies do you like?

B. I like comedies. How about you?

A. I don't like comedies very much. I like adventure movies.

B. Oh, I see.

A. Who's your favorite movie star?

B. Eddie Murphy. How about you?

A. Harrison Ford.

A. Tell me, _____ ?

B. Yes. I like to/like _____ a lot.

A. _____ do you like?

B. I like _____ . How about you?

A. I don't like _____ very much. I like _____ .

B. Oh, I see.

A. Who's your favorite _____ ?

B. _____ . How about you?

A. _____ .

You're taking a break at work and you and a co-worker are "making small talk." In the exercises below, talk with your co-worker about music, TV, and sports, using the model dialog above as a guide. Feel free to adapt and expand the model any way you wish.

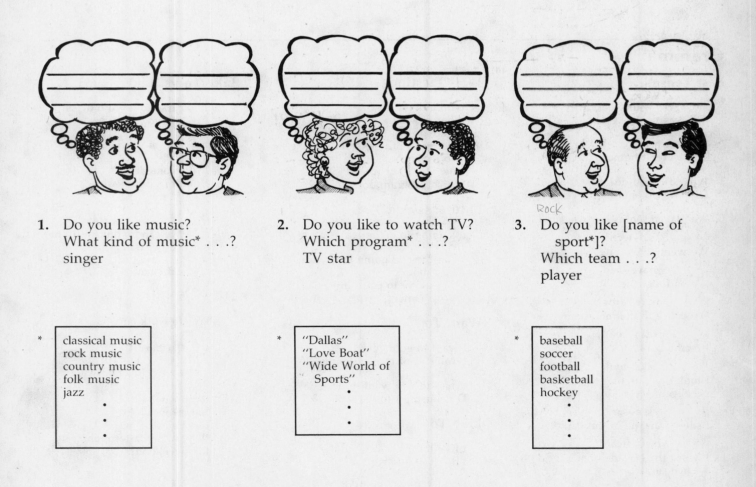

1. Do you like music?
   What kind of music* . . .?
   singer

2. Do you like to watch TV?
   Which program* . . .?
   TV star

3. Do you like [name of sport*]?
   Which team . . .?
   player

* classical music
  rock music
  country music
  folk music
  jazz
  •
  •
  •

* "Dallas"
  "Love Boat"
  "Wide World of
    Sports"
  •
  •
  •

* baseball
  soccer
  football
  basketball
  hockey
  •
  •
  •

Topic Vocabulary

Weather

cloudy
cold
hot
rain
snow
sunny

Sports

baseball
basketball
football
golf
hockey
jogging
sailing
skating
skiing
soccer
swimming
tennis

Recreation and Entertainment

ballgame
baseball stadium
beach
bike ride
concert
concert hall
county fair
dancing
dinner
garden
lake
mountains
movie (the movies)
museum
park
party
picnic
play
restaurant
river
theater
TV
walk
zoo

Movies

adventure movies
comedies
dramas
mysteries
science fiction movies
westerns

Music

classical music
country music
folk music
jazz
rock music

Performers

actor
actress
movie star
player
singer
TV star

Family Members

aunt
children
daughter
grandchildren
grandfather
grandmother
son
uncle
wife

Grammar

Past Tense

How **was** your weekend?
  It **was** very nice.

I **wasn't** home.
You **weren't** home.

What **did** you do?
Did you do anything special?

We play**ed** tennis last weekend.

   go—went
We **went** swimming.

   have—had
We **had** a picnic.

   drive—drove
We **drove** to the mountains.

   read—read
I **read** a book.

   take—took
I **took** my daughter to a ballgame.

   see—saw
I **saw** "Dancing in the Park."

   hear—heard
I **heard** the Philadelphia Orchestra.

WH-Questions

Who did you hear?
What movie did you see?
Where do you like to swim?
What kind of books do you like to read?
How was your weekend?
Which program do you like?

Future: Going To

It's **going to** be hot.

What are you **going to** do this weekend?
  I'm **going to** paint my apartment.

Want To

I **want to** go jogging.
I **don't want to** play tennis.

What do you **want to** do today?
Do you **want to** see a movie?

Like To

I **like to** run.
I **don't like to** run.

What do you **like to** do?
Do you **like to** run?

Like To vs. Like

Do you **like to** go to movies?
  I **like to** go to movies.

What kind of movies do you **like**?
  I **like** comedies.
  I **don't like** comedies.

Can

Maybe we **can** go out for dinner some other time.

I'm afraid I **can't**.

Have To

I **have to** work late.

Time Expressions

Do you want to go dancing
  tonight?
  tomorrow?
  tomorrow night?
  this Saturday **night**?
  this Sunday **afternoon**?
  this weekend?

Functions and Conversation Strategies in this chapter are listed in the Appendix, pages 198–199.

SCENES & IMPROVISATIONS
Chapters 7, 8, 9

Who do you think these people are?
What do you think they're talking about?
Create conversations based on these scenes and act them out.

1.

2.

3.

4.

5.

6.

7.

8.

- **HOUSING**
- **SOCIAL COMMUNICATION**
- **PERSONAL INFORMATION**

- Present Tense: Review • WH-Questions
- Yes/No Questions • Two-Word Verbs
- Past Tense: Review • Can • Could
- Should • Object Pronouns
- Possessive Adjectives • Time Expressions

Hello. I'm Your Neighbor
Is There a Laundromat in the Neighborhood?
Can I Park My Car Here?
Can I Help You Take Out the Garbage?
Could You Lend Me a Hammer?
I Knocked on Your Door Several Times Last Week
Maybe You Should Call a Plumber
Do You Fix Kitchen Sinks?

- Asking for and Reporting Information • Greeting People
- Attracting Attention • Gratitude • Appreciation
- Checking and Indicating Understanding • Initiating a Topic

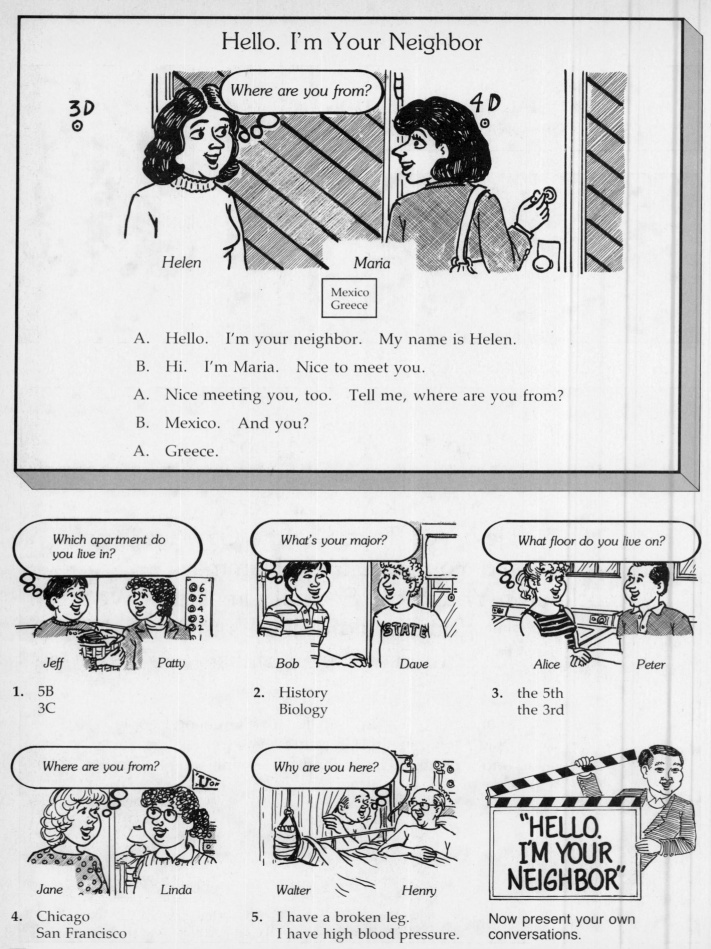

Hello. I'm Your Neighbor

Where are you from?

3D

4D

Helen   Maria

Mexico
Greece

A. Hello. I'm your neighbor. My name is Helen.

B. Hi. I'm Maria. Nice to meet you.

A. Nice meeting you, too. Tell me, where are you from?

B. Mexico. And you?

A. Greece.

Which apartment do you live in?

Jeff   Patty

1. 5B
    3C

What's your major?

Bob   Dave

2. History
    Biology

What floor do you live on?

Alice   Peter

3. the 5th
    the 3rd

Where are you from?

Jane   Linda

4. Chicago
    San Francisco

Why are you here?

Walter   Henry

5. I have a broken leg.
    I have high blood pressure.

"HELLO.
I'M YOUR
NEIGHBOR"

Now present your own conversations.

Is There a Laundromat in the Neighborhood?

> **Is there a laundromat in the neighborhood?**
>
> **Yes. There's a laundromat _around the corner._**

A. Excuse me.   I'm new here.   Can I ask you a question?

B. Sure.

A. Is there a laundromat in the neighborhood?

B. Yes.   There's a laundromat around the corner.

A. Around the corner?

B. Yes.

A. Thanks very much.

> Where's the bus stop?
>
> It's **down the block.**

1.

> Do they pick up the garbage today?
>
> No. They pick up the garbage **on Thursdays.**

2.

> What time does the mail come?
>
> At about **11 o'clock.**

3.

> Is there a supermarket nearby?
>
> Yes. There's a supermarket **on Pine Street.**

4.

> Where does the superintendent live?
>
> In the apartment **in the basement.**

5.

"IS THERE A LAUNDROMAT IN THE NEIGHBORHOOD?"

Now present your own conversations.

Can I Park My Car Here?

A. Pardon me. Can I ask you a question?

B. Certainly.

A. Can I park my car here?

B. Yes, you can.

A. Thanks.

A. Pardon me. Can I ask you a question?

B. Certainly.

A. Can I use my fireplace?

B. No, you can't.

A. Oh, okay. Thanks.

1.

2.

3.

4.

5.

Now present your own conversations.

Can I Help You Take Out the Garbage?

take out the garbage

A. Can I help you take out the garbage?

B. No. That's okay. I can take it out myself.

A. Please. Let me help you.

B. Well, all right. If you don't mind.

A. No, not at all.

B. Thanks. I appreciate it.

pick up your things

A. Can I help you pick up your things?

B. No. That's okay. I can pick them up myself.

A. Please. Let me help you.

B. Well, all right. If you don't mind.

A. No, not at all.

B. Thanks. I appreciate it.

1. hang up your laundry

2. put away these chairs

3. carry those bags

4. cut down that tree

5. clean up this mess

Now present your own conversations.

Could You Lend Me a Hammer?

lend me a hammer

A. Could I ask you a favor?

B. Yes.

A. Could you lend me a hammer?

B. All right.

A. Are you sure?

B. Yes. I'd be happy to lend you a hammer.

A. Thanks. I appreciate it.

1. help me start my car

2. lend me some flour

3. help me with my shopping bags

4. take care of Billy for a few minutes

5. pick up my mail while I'm away

"COULD YOU LEND ME A HAMMER?"

Now present your own conversations.

I Knocked on Your Door Several Times Last Week

A. You know, I knocked on your door several times last week, but you weren't home.

B. No, I wasn't. I was in Detroit.

A. Oh. What did you do there?

B. I visited my daughter and her husband.

A. Oh. That's nice.

Now present your own conversations.

* come–came
  ring–rang

Maybe You Should Call a Plumber

A. What are you doing?

B. I'm trying to fix my kitchen sink.

A. What's wrong with it?

B. It's leaking.

A. I see.   And you're trying to fix it yourself?

B. Yes.   But I'm having a lot of trouble.

A. You know, maybe you should call a plumber.

B. Hmm.   You're probably right.

1. call an electrician

2. call a carpenter

3. call the gas company

4. call the superintendent

5. call a plumber

Now present your own conversations.

INTERCHANGE
Do You Fix Kitchen Sinks?

A. Ace Plumbing Company.

B. Hello. Do you fix kitchen sinks?

A. Yes. What's the problem?

B. My kitchen sink is leaking.

A. I see. We can send a plumber at two o'clock this afternoon. Is that okay?

B. Two o'clock this afternoon? Yes, that's fine.

A. Okay. What's the name?

B. Eric Jensen.

A. Spell the last name, please.

B. J-E-N-S-E-N.

A. And the address?

B. 93 Cliff Street.

A. Phone number?

B. 972-3053.

A. All right. A plumber will be there at two o'clock this afternoon.

B. Thank you.

A. _____.

B. Hello. Do you fix _____s?

A. Yes. What's the problem?

B. _____.

A. I see. We can send a _____ at _____. Is that okay?

B. _____? Yes, that's fine.

A. Okay. What's the name?

B. _____.

A. Spell the last name, please.

B. _____.

A. And the address?

B. _____.

A. Phone number?

B. _____.

A. All right. A _____ will be there at _____.

B. Thank you.

Something in your home is broken. Call a plumber, a carpenter, or an electrician, using the model dialog above as a guide. Feel free to adapt and expand the model any way you wish.

Topic Vocabulary

Housing

apartment
balcony
basement
building
doorbell
fireplace
floor
front door
garbage
garbage bags
garden
laundry
mail
neighbor
superintendent

Community

bus stop
laundromat
mail
supermarket

Household Fixtures and Appliances

kitchen sink
light
oven
radiator
stove
toilet

Household Repairs

carpenter
electrician
gas company
plumber

Personal Information

address
last name
name
phone number

Family Members

cousin
daughter
grandchildren
husband
son

Grammar

Simple Present Tense: Review

am	I**'m** your neighbor.
is	My name **is** Helen.
are	Where **are** you from?
do	Which apartment **do** you live in?
does	What time **does** the mail come?

WH-Questions

What's your major?
Where are you from?
Why are you here?
Which apartment do you live in?

Yes/No Questions

Is there a laundromat in the neighborhood?

Do they pick up the garbage today?

Two-Word Verbs

clean up this mess – **clean** it **up**
cut down that tree – **cut** it **down**
hang up your laundry – **hang** it **up**
pick up your things – **pick** them **up**
put away those chairs – **put** them **away**
take out the garbage – **take** it **out**

Past Tense: Review

I **was** in Detroit.
I **wasn't.**
You **weren't** home.

I visit**ed** my daughter.

I **saw** a Broadway show.
I **drove** through the Rocky Mountains.
I **took** care of my grandchildren.
I **went** to Disneyland.

come–came
I **came** by.

ring–rang
I **rang** your doorbell.

Can

Can I park my car here?
Yes, you **can.**
No, you **can't.**

Can I help you take out the garbage?
I **can** take it out myself.

Could

Could I ask you a favor?

Should

Maybe you **should** call a plumber.

Object Pronouns

Could you lend **me** a hammer?
I'd be happy to lend **you** a hammer.

Possessive Adjectives

Could you help me start **my** car?
I'd be happy to help you start **your** car.

Time Expressions

We can send a plumber **at two o'clock this afternoon.**

Functions and Conversation Strategies in this chapter are listed in the Appendix, **pages 199–200.**

11

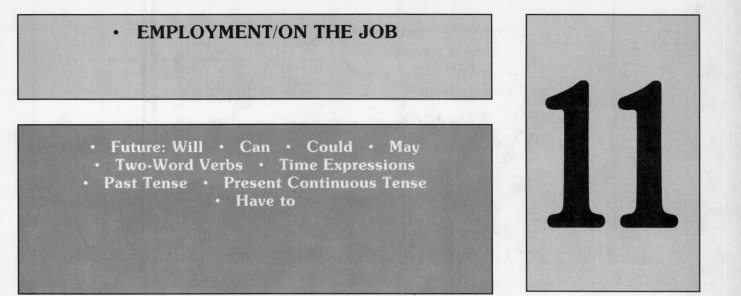

- Future: Will · Can · Could · May
- Two-Word Verbs · Time Expressions
- Past Tense · Present Continuous Tense
- Have to

Could You Please Hand Me a Screwdriver?
Could You Possibly Type This Letter?
Do You Want Me to Give Out the Paychecks?
I'm Not Busy Right Now. Do You Want Any Help?
I Apologize
I'm Sorry I Was Late for Work This Morning
May I Please Leave at 4:00 Today?
Could I Possibly Take the Day Off Tomorrow?

- Requests · Permission · Offering to Do Something
- Offering to Help · Apologizing · Obligation
- Checking and Indicating Understanding · Hesitating

Could You Please Hand Me a Screwdriver?

A. Could you please hand me a screwdriver?

B. A screwdriver? Okay.

A. Thanks.

B. You're welcome.

1.

2.

3.

4.

5.

Now present your own conversations.

Could You Possibly Type This Letter?

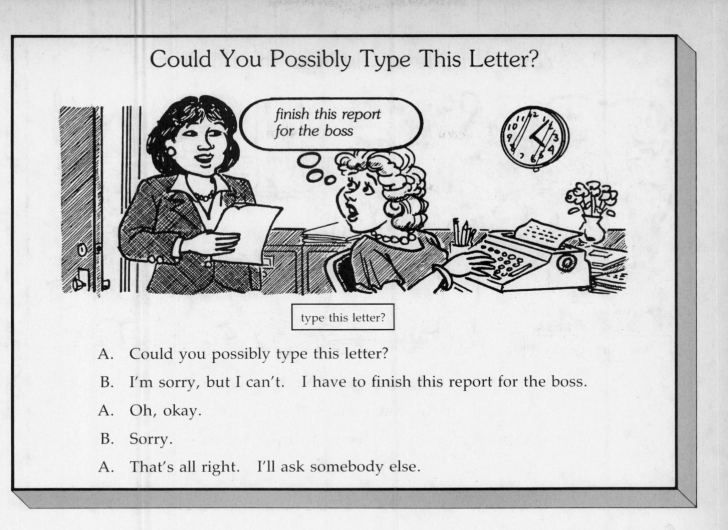

finish this report for the boss

type this letter?

A. Could you possibly type this letter?

B. I'm sorry, but I can't.   I have to finish this report for the boss.

A. Oh, okay.

B. Sorry.

A. That's all right.   I'll ask somebody else.

make these copies before 5 o'clock

1. mail these packages this afternoon?

go to a meeting at my son's school

2. work overtime tomorrow?

take these boxes to the warehouse

3. help me load the truck?

pick up my sister at the airport

4. give me a ride home?

take these bags to the front entrance

5. take Mr. and Mrs. Brown's luggage to Room 418?

"COULD YOU POSSIBLY TYPE THIS LETTER?"

Now present your own conversations.

Do You Want Me to Give Out the Paychecks?

give out the paychecks?

A. Do you want me to give out the paychecks?

B. Yes.   If you don't mind.

A. Not at all.   I'll be happy to give them out.

B. Thanks.   I really appreciate it.

1. hang up the new calendar?

2. put away these glasses?

3. sort the mail?

4. set up the meeting room?

5. bag these groceries?

"DO YOU WANT ME TO GIVE OUT THE PAYCHECKS?"

Now present your own conversations.

I'm Not Busy Right Now. Do You Want Any Help?

clean up the stockroom

A. I'm not busy right now. Do you want any help?

B. I don't think so. I'm just cleaning up the stockroom.

A. I'll be glad to help you clean it up.

B. Well, okay. It's nice of you to offer.

A. My pleasure.

1. take out the trash

2. file some reports

3. fold these towels

4. take down this sign

5. put up these decorations

Now present your own conversations.

I Apologize

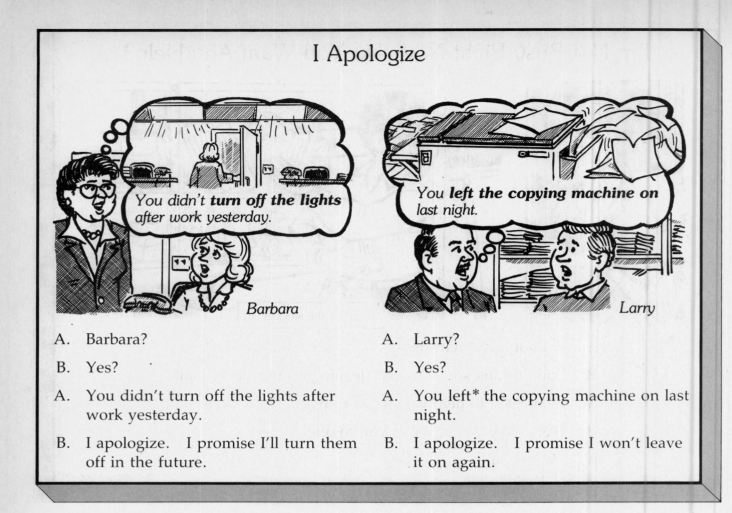

Barbara

Larry

A. Barbara?

B. Yes?

A. You didn't turn off the lights after work yesterday.

B. I apologize. I promise I'll turn them off in the future.

A. Larry?

B. Yes?

A. You left* the copying machine on last night.

B. I apologize. I promise I won't leave it on again.

1. Frank

2. Howard

3. Ms. Powers

4. Mr. Hinkel

5. Henry

Now present your own conversations.

* leave—left

I'm Sorry I Was Late for Work This Morning

I missed the bus.

He was late for work this morning.

A. I'm sorry I was late for work this morning.

B. That's all right.

A. The reason is that I missed the bus.

B. I understand. Don't worry about it.

I had a bad headache.

1. She didn't come to work yesterday.

I went out the back door and forgot about the lights.

2. He left the lights on last night.

I had a flat tire on the way to work.

3. She missed the meeting this morning.

I was in a hurry to leave because I had a dentist appointment.

4. He forgot to lock the cash register yesterday evening.

I didn't remember the instructions.

5. He broke* the ice cream machine.

"I'M SORRY I WAS LATE FOR WORK THIS MORNING"

Now present your own conversations.

* break–broke

May I Please Leave at 4:00 Today?

A. May I please leave at 4:00 today?

B. At 4:00?

A. Yes.   Is that all right with you?

B. Hmm.   Well . . . I guess so.

A. Thank you.

1.

2.

3.

4.

5.

Now present your own
conversations.

Could I Possibly Take the Day Off Tomorrow?

A. Excuse me, Mrs. Clark.

B. Yes?

A. Could I possibly take the day off tomorrow?

B. Hmm.   I don't think so.

A. I see.   Uh . . . the reason I asked is my husband is going into the hospital tomorrow for an operation.

B. Oh, I understand.   Well, in that case, I suppose you can take the day off tomorrow.

A. Thank you very much.

A. Excuse me, (Mr./Mrs./Ms./Miss) _____.

B. Yes?

A. Could I possibly _____?

B. Hmm.   I don't think so.

A. I see.   Uh . . . the reason I asked is _____
_____.

B. Oh, I understand.   Well, in that case, I suppose you can _____
_____.

A. Thank you very much.

You're asking your employer for permission to do something.   Create an original conversation using the model dialog above as a guide.   Feel free to adapt and expand the model any way you wish.

CHAPTER 11 SUMMARY

Topic Vocabulary

Objects on the Job

box
calendar
cash register
copies
copying machine
cup
decorations
desk
glass
groceries
letter
lights
line
luggage
machine
mail
napkin
package
paycheck
report
screwdriver
sign
table
tools
towel
trash

truck
window

Job Procedures

bag *these groceries*
clean up *table 12*
come in *late*
file *some reports*
finish *this report*
fold *these towels*
get *napkins*
give out *the paychecks*
hand me *a screwdriver*
hang up *the calendar*
help me
leave *the copying machine* on
load *the truck*
lock *the cash register*
mail *these packages*
make *5 copies*
punch in
put away *these glasses*
put up *these decorations*
set up *the meeting room*
sort *the mail*
spell *my name*
take down *this sign*

take out *the trash*
take *the day* off
take *this package*
transfer *this call*
turn off *the lights*
type *this letter*

Places on the Job

back door
front entrance
meeting room
Room *418*
Shipping Department
stockroom
supply room
warehouse

Additional Employment Vocabulary

boss
day off
employer
instructions
late
meeting
overtime
vacation

Grammar

Future: Will

I'll ask somebody else.
I'll be happy to give them out.

I **won't** leave it on again.

Can

I suppose you **can** take the day off tomorrow.

I'm sorry, but I **can't**.

Could

Could you please hand me a screwdriver?
Could I possibly take the day off tomorrow?

May

May I please leave at 4:00?

Two-Word Verbs

clean up the stockroom – **clean** it **up**
give out the paychecks – **give** them **out**
hang up the calendar – **hang** it **up**
put away these glasses – **put** them **away**
put up these decorations – **put** them **up**
set up the meeting room – **set** it **up**
take down this sign – **take** it **down**
take out the trash – **take** it **out**

Time Expressions

You didn't turn off the lights
 last night.
 this morning.
 today.
 yesterday.

May I please leave **at 4:00 today**?
May I please take the day off **tomorrow**?
May I please come in late **tomorrow morning**?
May I please take **next Monday** off?
May I please take my vacation **in July**?

Past Tense

I'm sorry I **was** late.

You **didn't** turn off the lights.

break–broke
I **broke** the ice cream machine.

forget–forgot
You **forgot** to punch in this morning.

leave–left
You **left** the copying machine on last night.

Present Continuous Tense

I'm clean**ing** up the stockroom.

Have To

I **have to** finish this report.

Functions and Conversation Strategies in this chapter are listed in the Appendix, **page 200.**

• TELEPHONE • TRANSPORTATION • EMERGENCIES

• Imperatives • Prepositions of Location
• Future: Will • Time Expressions
• Past Tense • WH-Questions • May
• Could • Want to • Possessive Adjectives
• Object Pronouns

Could You Please Tell Me How to Make a
Long Distance Call?
I Want to Make This a Collect Call, Please
May I Please Speak to Betty?
When Is the Next Bus to Buffalo?
Please Fasten Your Seat Belt!
I Want to Report an Emergency!

• Asking for and Reporting Information • Instructing
• Identifying • Requests • Checking and Indicating Understanding
• Asking for Repetition • Initiating Conversations

Could You Please Tell Me How to Make a Long Distance Call?

make a long distance call

A. Excuse me. Could you please tell me how to make a long distance call?

B. Sure. Dial "one." Dial the area code. Then, dial the local phone number. Have you got it?

A. I think so. Let me see. I dial "one." I dial the area code. And then I . . . hmm. Could you repeat the last step?

B. Yes. Dial the local phone number.

A. Okay. I understand. Thanks very much.

A. Excuse me. Could you please tell me how to _____?

B. Sure. _____.
_____.
Then, _____.
Have you got it?

A. I think so. Let me see. I _____.
I _____.
And then I . . . hmm. Could you repeat the last step?

B. Yes. _____.

A. Okay. I understand. Thanks very much.

- *Pick up the receiver.*
- *Put the money in the coin slot.*
- *Dial the number.*

1. use this pay phone

- *Dial "zero."*
- *Dial the area code and local phone number.*
- *Tell the operator it's a collect call and give your name.*

2. make a collect call

- *Dial "zero."*
- *Dial the area code and local phone number.*
- *Tell the operator it's a person-to-person call and give the name of the person you're calling.*

3. make a person-to-person call

"COULD YOU PLEASE TELL ME HOW TO MAKE A LONG DISTANCE CALL?"

Now present your own conversations.

I Want to Make This a Collect Call, Please

A. Operator.

B. I want to make this a collect call, please.

A. What's your name?

B. Edward Bratt.

A. Did you say Edward Pratt?

B. No. Edward Bratt.

A. All right. One moment, please.

1. make this a person-to-person call

2. make this a collect call

3. make this a person-to-person call

4. make this a person-to-person collect call to Rose Wilson

5. charge this to my home phone

Now present your own conversations.

May I Please Speak to Betty?

Betty?

her friend Steve

in an hour

A. May I please speak to Betty?

B. I'm afraid she isn't here right now.

A. Oh, I see.   When will she be back?

B. She'll probably be back in an hour.   May I ask who's calling?

A. This is her friend Steve.

B. Do you want to leave a message?

A. Yes.   Please ask her to call me when she gets back.

B. All right.   I'll give her the message.

A. Thank you.

Mr. Green?

his brother, Harold

in a few minutes

1.

Mrs. Quinn?

her husband

in a few hours

2.

Abdul?

in 2 or 3 hours

Carlos, from his English class

3.

Mr. or Mrs. Benson?

their lawyer, Ms. Kramer

in a little while

4.

Mr. Jenkins?

Bob Hill, in Apartment 3B

in about an hour

5.

"MAY I PLEASE SPEAK TO BETTY?"

Now present your own conversations.

When Is the Next Bus to Buffalo?

A. When is the next bus to Buffalo?

B. It's at 4:10.*

A. At 4:10?

B. Yes.

A. I'd like a round-trip ticket, please.

B. All right.　That'll be twenty-four dollars and fifty cents ($24.50).

1.

train to Cleveland? — 2:37*
a one-way ticket — $38.75

2.

flight to Los Angeles? — 10:55*
2 one-way tickets — $360

3.

train to Chattanooga? — 6:25*
2 round-trip tickets — $86.90

4.

bus to El Paso? — 3:07†
round-trip tickets for two adults and two children — $92.70

5.

boat to the Statue of Liberty? — 11:05†
23 tickets — $34.50

"WHEN IS THE NEXT BUS TO BUFFALO?"

Now present your own conversations.

---

* 4:10 = four ten
 2:37 = two thirty-seven
 10:55 = ten fifty-five
 6:25 = six twenty-five

† 3:07 = three "oh" seven
 11:05 = eleven "oh" five

Please Fasten Your Seat Belt!

A. Excuse me. Please fasten your seat belt!

B. I'm sorry. I didn't hear you. What did you say?

A. I said, "Please fasten your seat belt!"

B. Oh, okay.

1.

2.

3.

4.

5.

Now present your own conversations.

INTERCHANGE
I Want to Report an Emergency!

A car just hit a pedestrian.

Diane Lockwood

on Washington Street between *Second and Third Avenue*

A. Police.

B. I want to report an emergency!

A. Yes. Go ahead.

B. A car just hit* a pedestrian.

A. Where?

B. On Washington Street between Second and Third Avenue.

A. Did you say Second and Third Avenue?

B. Yes. That's right.

A. What's your name?

B. Diane Lockwood.

A. All right. We'll be there right away.

* hit–hit

A. Police.

B. I want to report an emergency!

A. Yes. Go ahead.

B. _____ .

A. Where?

B. _____ .

A. Did you say _____?

B. Yes. That's right.

A. What's your name?

B. _____ .

A. All right. We'll be there right away.

1. at the corner of *Broadway and K Street*

2. in front of *the Hilton Hotel*

3. in the parking lot on *Maple Street*

4. near *the statue of Robert E. Lee*

You're reporting an emergency. Create an original conversation using the model dialog above as a guide. Feel free to adapt and expand the model any way you wish.

CHAPTER 12 SUMMARY

Topic Vocabulary

Telephone

area code
coin slot
collect call
home phone
local phone number
long distance call
message
number
operator
pay phone
person-to-person call
receiver

charge
dial

Transportation

boat
bus
flight
train

ticket
one-way ticket
round-trip ticket

cars
door
seat
seat belt
white line

fasten
lean
ride
smoke
stand

Emergencies

accident
emergency
heart attack
pedestrian

hit
mug
report
rob

Grammar

Imperatives

Dial "one."
Dial the area code.
Then, dial the local phone number.

Please fasten your seat belt!
Please don't smoke on the bus!

Prepositions of Location

Please don't lean **against** the doors!
At the corner of Broadway and K Street.
Please stand **behind** the white line.
Please don't ride **between** the cars.
Between Second and Third Avenue.
In the parking lot.
In front of the Hilton Hotel.
Near the statue.
Please don't smoke **on** the bus!
On Washington Street.
Please put your bag **under** the seat **in front of** you.

Future: Will

When **will** he   be back?
        she
         they

He**'ll**   be back in an hour.
She**'ll**
They**'ll**

Time Expressions

She'll be back **in an hour.**
             in about an hour.
             in 2 or 3 hours.
             in a few hours.
             in a few minutes.
             in a little while.

It's **at** 4:10 (four ten).
It's **at** 3:07 (three "oh" seven).

Past Tense

hit–hit
A car just **hit** a pedestrian.

say–said
I **said**, "Please fasten your seat belt!"

Somebody just robb**ed** a grocery store.

WH-Questions

Who are you calling?
What's your name?

May

May I please speak to Betty?

Could

Could you please tell me how to make a long distance call?

Want To

I **want to** make this a collect call, please.

Possessive Adjectives

This is **her** friend Steve.
This is **his** brother, Harold.
This is **their** lawyer, Ms. Kramer.

Object Pronouns

Please ask **her**   to call **me.**
         him
         them

Functions and Conversation Strategies in this chapter are listed in the Appendix, **pages 200–201.**

SCENES & IMPROVISATIONS
Chapters 10, 11, 12

Who do you think these people are?
What do you think they're talking about?
Create conversations based on these scenes and act them out.

1.

2.

3.

4.

5.

6.

7.

8.

• Partitives • Would • Count/Non-Count Nouns
• Imperatives • May • Adjectives

Do We Need Anything from the Supermarket?
What Do You Want Me to Get?
I Want a Pound of Roast Beef
Your Change Is $2.75
I'd Like a Hamburger and an Order of French Fries
I'd Like the Chicken
Would You Like a Few More Meatballs?
Can You Tell Me the Recipe?

• Want–Desire • Complimenting • Requests
• Preference • Instructing • Persuading–Insisting
• Checking and Indicating Understanding • Hesitating

Do We Need Anything from the Supermarket?

A. Do we need anything from the supermarket?

B. Yes. We need a quart of milk.

A. A quart?

B. Yes.

A. Anything else?

B. No, I don't think so.

A. Okay. I'll get a quart of milk.

B. Thanks.

a quart of milk

a pound of apples

1.

a gallon of orange juice

2.

2 boxes of rice

3.

a dozen eggs

4.

2 jars of mayonnaise

5.

"DO WE NEED ANYTHING FROM THE SUPERMARKET?"

Now present your own conversations.

What Do You Want Me to Get?

A. Could you do me a favor?

B. Sure. What is it?

A. We need a few things from the supermarket.

B. What do you want me to get?

A. A can of tuna fish, a loaf of white bread, and a head of lettuce.

B. A can of tuna fish, a loaf of white bread, and a head of lettuce. Anything else?

A. No. That's all. Thanks.

1.
a dozen oranges | a pound of butter | a bunch of bananas

2.
a gallon of skim milk | a bottle of ketchup | a jar of mayonnaise

3.
a bag of potato chips | 2 loaves of whole wheat bread | half a gallon of apple juice

4.
a pint of vanilla ice cream | half a dozen eggs | 2 bunches of grapes

5.
a jar of peanut butter | a quart of chocolate milk | a box of chocolate chip cookies

"WHAT DO YOU WANT ME TO GET?"

Now present your own conversations.

I Want a Pound of Roast Beef

A. May I help you?

B. Yes, please. I want a pound of roast beef.

A. Anything else?

B. Yes. A dozen rolls.

A. All right. That's a pound of roast beef and a dozen rolls. Is that it?

B. Yes. That's it.

1.

2.

3.

4.

5.

Now present your own conversations.

Your Change is $2.75

A. That'll be seven twenty-five ($7.25).

B. Seven twenty-five?

A. Yes.

B. Here's ten ($10).

A. All right.   Your change is two dollars and seventy-five cents ($2.75). Here you are.

B. Thank you.

A. Have a nice day.

1. $1.15

2. $3.57

3. $8.40

4. $6.08

5. $.02

Now present your own conversations.

I'd Like a Hamburger and an Order of French Fries

A. Welcome to Burger King. May I help you?

B. Yes. I'd like a hamburger and an order of french fries.

A. Do you want anything to drink with that?

B. Yes. I'll have a cup of coffee.

A. Okay. That's a hamburger, an order of french fries, and a cup of coffee. Is that for here or to go?

B. For here.

A. That comes to two dollars and ninety cents ($2.90), please.

B. Here you are.

A. And here's your change. Your food will be ready in a moment.

for here
$2.90

1. to go
$2.65

2. for here
$4.10

3. to go
$5.05

4. for here
$4.80

5. to go
$27.94

"I'D LIKE A HAMBURGER AND AN ORDER OF FRENCH FRIES"

Now present your own conversations.

I'd Like the Chicken

the chicken · a baked potato · a glass of milk

rice or a baked potato?

A. What would you like?

B. I'd like the chicken.

A. All right. And would you prefer rice or a baked potato with that?

B. I'd prefer a baked potato.

A. And would you like anything to drink?

B. Yes. Let me see . . . I'll have a glass of milk.

A. Okay. That's the chicken with a baked potato, and a glass of milk.

the fish · noodles · a cup of coffee

1. noodles or rice?

the meat loaf · mashed potatoes · a Pepsi

2. french fries or mashed potatoes?

the lamb chops · spaghetti · a cup of tea

3. spaghetti or rice?

the roast beef · rice · a glass of wine

4. rice or a baked potato?

the "special of the day" · baked beans · an iced tea

5. noodles or baked beans?

"I'D LIKE THE CHICKEN"

Now present your own conversations.

Would You Like a Few More Meatballs?

meatballs

salad

A. Would you like a few more meatballs?

B. They're delicious . . . but no, thank you.

A. Oh, come on!   Have a few more.

B. All right,   But, please . . . not too many.

A. Would you like a little more salad?

B. It's very good . . . but no, thank you.

A. Oh, come on!   Have a little more.

B. All right.   But, please . . . not too much.

1. mushrooms

2. ice cream

3. cake

4. cookies

5. pie

Now present your own conversations.

INTERCHANGE
Can You Tell Me the Recipe?

A. Your cake was delicious. Can you tell me the recipe?

B. Sure. First, mix together a cup of flour, a teaspoon of salt, and two tablespoons of water.

A. I see.

B. Then, add half a cup of sugar. Are you with me so far?

A. Yes. I'm following you.

B. Okay. Next, add two eggs.

A. Uh-húh.

B. And then, put the mixture into a baking pan and bake for one hour at 350 degrees. Have you got all that?

A. Yes, I've got it. Thanks.

A. Your _____ was delicious. Can you tell me the recipe?

B. Sure. First, _____.

A. I see.

B. Then, _____.
Are you with me so far?

A. Yes. I'm following you.

B. Okay. Next, _____.

A. Uh-húh.

B. And then, _____.
Have you got all that?

A. Yes, I've got it. Thanks.

You're a dinner guest at somebody's home. Compliment the host or hostess and ask for a recipe, using the model dialog above as a guide. Feel free to adapt and expand the model any way you wish.

Topic Vocabulary

Food Items

apple
banana
beans
   baked beans
   refried beans
beef
   ground beef
bread
   white bread
   whole wheat bread
butter
cake
cheese
   American cheese
   Swiss cheese
cheeseburger
chicken
coffee
cole slaw
cookies
   chocolate chip cookies
doughnut
egg
fish
flour
grapes
hamburger
hot dog
ice cream
   vanilla ice cream
juice
   apple juice
ketchup
lamb chop

lemonade
lettuce
mayonnaise
meatballs
meat loaf
milk
   chocolate milk
   skim milk
mushrooms
mustard
noodles
orange
orange juice
peanut butter
pie
potato
   baked potato
   french fries
   mashed potatoes
potato chips
potato salad
rice
roast beef
rolls
salad
salt
sandwich
   fish sandwich
   roast beef sandwich
shake
   chocolate shake
soda
   Coke
   orange soda
   Pepsi
spaghetti

sugar
taco
tea
   iced tea
tuna fish
water
wine

Food Units

bag
bottle
box
bunch
can
dozen
gallon
head
jar
loaf–loaves
piece
pint
pound
quart

half a cup
half a dozen
half a gallon
half a pound

tablespoon
teaspoon

container
cup
glass

order
piece

small
medium
large

Purchasing Food

change
for here
"special of the day"
to go

Describing Food

delicious
excellent
fantastic
very good

Recipes

add
bake
baking pan
350 degrees
mix together
mixture
recipe

Grammar

Partitives

a bag of potato chips
a box of rice
a bottle of ketchup
a bunch of bananas
a can of tuna fish
a container of cole slaw
a cup of coffee
a dozen eggs
a gallon of orange juice
a glass of milk
a head of lettuce
a jar of mayonnaise
a loaf of bread
an order of french fries
a piece of chicken
a pint of ice cream
a pound of apples
a quart of milk

half a dozen eggs

half a gallon of apple juice
half a pound of cheese

a cup of flour
a tablespoon of water
a teaspoon of salt

Would

What **would** you like?
Would you prefer rice or a
   baked potato?

I'd like the chicken.
I'd prefer a baked potato.

Count/Non-Count Nouns

Count
Would you like **a few** more
   meatballs?
Have **a few** more.

They're delicious.
Not **too many.**

Non-Count
Would you like **a little** more
   salad?
Have **a little** more.

It's very good.
Not **too much.**

Imperatives

Add half a cup of sugar.

May

May I help you?

Adjectives

They're **delicious.**

Functions and Conversation Strategies in this chapter are listed in the Appendix, pages 201–202.

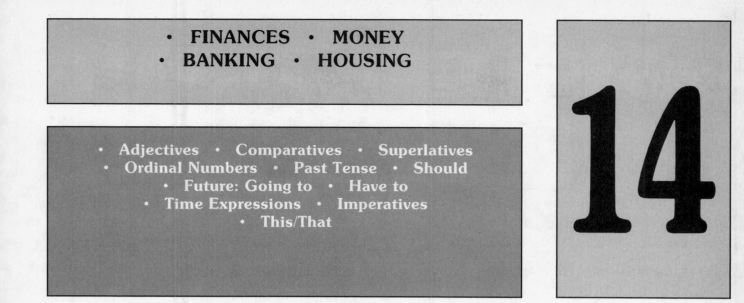

• FINANCES • MONEY
• BANKING • HOUSING

14

• Adjectives • Comparatives • Superlatives
• Ordinal Numbers • Past Tense • Should
• Future: Going to • Have to
• Time Expressions • Imperatives
• This/That

I Don't Think We Can Afford It
Can You Show Me a Less Expensive One?
I Think We Should Stop at the Bank
I'd Like to Deposit This in My Savings Account
I'm Balancing the Checkbook
Why Are You Banging on the Vending Machine?
Did You Remember to Pay the Telephone Bill?
I Think There's a Mistake on My Electric Bill

• Remembering/Forgetting • Describing
• Agreement/Disagreement • Certainty/Uncertainty
• Advice–Suggestions • Checking and Indicating Understanding
• Initiating a Topic

I Don't Think We Can Afford It

refrigerator
large

A. Which refrigerator do you like?

B. I like this one.   It's very large.

A. I know.   It's larger than that one, but it's also more expensive.

B. Hmm.   You're right.

A. I don't think we can afford it.

B. I suppose not.

sofa
comfortable

A. Which sofa do you like?

B. I like this one.   It's very comfortable.

A. I know.   It's more comfortable than that one, but it's also more expensive.

B. Hmm.   You're right.

A. I don't think we can afford it.

B. I suppose not.

1. air conditioner
   quiet

2. rug
   attractive

3. crib
   nice

4. stereo system
   good*

5. computer
   powerful

"I DON'T THINK WE CAN AFFORD IT"

Now present your own
conversations.

* good–better

Can You Show Me a Less Expensive One?

a firm mattress
$300

A. May I help you?

B. Yes. I'm looking for a firm mattress.

A. Take a look at this one. It's the firmest mattress in the store.

B. How much is it?

A. Three hundred dollars ($300).

B. I see. Can you show me a less expensive one?

A. Certainly. I'll be happy to.

a comfortable armchair
$450

A. May I help you?

B. Yes. I'm looking for a comfortable armchair.

A. Take a look at this one. It's the most comfortable armchair in the store.

B. How much is it?

A. Four hundred and fifty dollars ($450).

B. I see. Can you show me a less expensive one?

A. Certainly. I'll be happy to.

1. a large kitchen table
$225

2. a lightweight typewriter
$185

3. a big bookcase
$540

4. a good* cassette player
$160

5. a powerful computer
$3,750

Now present your own conversations.

* good–best

I Think We Should Stop at the Bank

buy stamps at the post office
take the kids to the zoo tomorrow

A. You know . . . I think we should stop at the bank.

B. Why? Do we need cash?

A. Yes. Remember . . . We have to buy stamps at the post office, and we're going to take the kids to the zoo tomorrow.

B. You're right. I forgot. How much do you think we should get?

A. I think forty dollars ($40) will be enough.

B. I think so, too.

1. buy food for the
   weekend
   see a movie tonight

2. pay the baby-sitter
   go out for dinner
   tomorrow night

3. buy a birthday present
   for Uncle Bob
   drive to the beach
   tomorrow

4. get an anniversary gift
   for your parents
   visit my sister in New
   York on Sunday

5. get more dog food for
   Rover
   go skiing this weekend

Now present your own
conversations.

I'd Like to Deposit This in My Savings Account

A. I'd like to deposit this in my savings account.

B. All right. Please print your name on the deposit slip.

A. Oh. Did I forget to print my name on the deposit slip?

B. Yes, you did.

A. Sorry.

1.

2.

3.

4.

5.

Now present your own conversations.

I'm Balancing the Checkbook

A. What are you doing?

B. I'm balancing the checkbook.

A. Oh.   I forgot to tell you.   I wrote a check to Dr. Anderson for Billy's examination.

B. Oh.   Do you remember the amount?

A. Yes.   Seventy-five dollars ($75).

B. Okay.   Thanks.

1.

Pay to the order of *Tyler's Department Store* $130 XX/100
One hundred thirty and XX/100 — Dollars
Memo   *new curtains*   *Betty Hunter*
Nov. 22 19

2.

Pay to the order of *Empire Clothing* $44 00/100
Forty-four and 00/100 — Dollars
Memo   *2 shirts and a tie*   *Peter G. Brown*
Dec. 18 19

3.

Pay to the order of *Phil's Pharmacy* $17 XX/100
Seventeen and XX/100 — Dollars
Memo   *Medicine and Vitamins*   *Karen W. Lee*
Oct. 30 19

4.

Pay to the order of *Lakeside Hospital* $60 00/100
Sixty and 00/100 — Dollars
Memo   *Janet's X-rays*   *William Stone*
6/11 19

5.

Pay to the order of *Rockwell University* $6,500 XX/100
Six thousand five hundred and XX/100 Dollars
Memo   *This year's tuition*   *Sara Thomas*
2/10 19

"I'M BALANCING THE CHECKBOOK"

Now present your own conversations.

Why Are You Banging on the Vending Machine?

A. Why are you banging on the vending machine?

B. I'm trying to buy soda, but I just lost* my money.

A. What did you put* in?

B. A quarter and a dime.†

A. Thirty-five cents? That's too bad! You should call the number on the machine and ask for your money back.

B. I will.

† a penny
1 cent

a nickel
5 cents

a dime
10 cents

a quarter
25 cents

1.

2.

3.

4.

5.

Now present your own conversations.

* lose–lost
  put–put

145

Did You Remember to Pay the Telephone Bill?

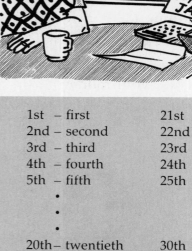

A. Did you remember to pay the telephone bill?

B. The telephone bill? That isn't due yet.

A. Are you sure?

B. Yes. I'm positive. Look! Here's the bill. It's due on January 10th.*

A. Oh, okay.

*					
January	(JAN)	July	(JUL)	1st – first	21st – twenty-first
February	(FEB)	August	(AUG)	2nd – second	22nd – twenty-second
March	(MAR)	September	(SEPT)	3rd – third	23rd – twenty-third
April	(APR)	October	(OCT)	4th – fourth	24th – twenty-fourth
May	(MAY)	November	(NOV)	5th – fifth	25th – twenty-fifth
June	(JUN)	December	(DEC)	•	•
				•	•
				•	•
				20th – twentieth	30th – thirtieth

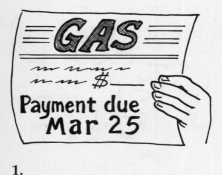

1.

2.

3.

4.

5.

Now present your own conversations.

INTERCHANGE
I Think There's a Mistake on My Electric Bill

A. Southeast Electric Company.   May I help you?

B. Yes.   I think there's a mistake on my electric bill.

A. Oh.   What's the problem?

B. I believe I was charged too much.

A. I see.   What is your name?

B. John Lawson.

A. And your account number?

B. 463 21 0978.

A. And what is the amount on your bill?

B. Four hundred and thirty dollars ($430).

A. All right.   Please hold and I'll check our records.

B. Thank you.

A. _____.   May I help you?

B. Yes.   I think there's a mistake on my _____ bill.

A. Oh.   What's the problem?

B. I believe I was charged too much.

A. I see.   What is your name?

B. _____.

A. And your account number?

B. _____.

A. And what is the amount on your bill?

B. _____.

A. All right.   Please hold and I'll check our records.

B. Thank you.

There is a mistake on one of your utility bills (electric, gas, telephone, oil, water, cable TV). Call the company and tell them about the mistake, using the model dialog above as a guide.   Feel free to adapt and expand the model any way you wish.

CHAPTER 14 SUMMARY

Topic Vocabulary

Furniture

armchair
bookcase
crib
kitchen table
mattress
rug
sofa

Department Store Items

cassette player
computer
stereo system
typewriter

Household Fixtures and Appliances

air conditioner
refrigerator

Describing

attractive
big
comfortable
expensive
firm
good
large
lightweight
nice
powerful
quiet

Finances

afford
balance
buy
pay

cash
check
checkbook
money

Banking

cash *this* check
deposit
endorse
make a withdrawal
print *your name*
sign *your name*

account number
amount
check
checking account
deposit slip
savings account
withdrawal slip

Coins

penny   –   1 cent
nickel –   5 cents
dime   – 10 cents
quarter – 25 cents

Utility Bills

cable TV bill
electric bill
gas bill
oil bill
telephone bill
water bill

account number
amount
due

Months of the Year

January	(JAN)
February	(FEB)
March	(MAR)
April	(APR)
May	(MAY)
June	(JUN)
July	(JUL)
August	(AUG)
September	(SEPT)
October	(OCT)
November	(NOV)
December	(DEC)

Grammar

Adjectives

It's very **large**.

I'm looking for a **firm** mattress.

Comparatives

It's **quieter** than that one.
It's **larger** than that one.

It's **more comfortable** than that one.

It's **better** than that one.

Superlatives

It's **the firmest** mattress in the store.
It's **the largest** kitchen table in the store.
It's **the biggest** bookcase in the store.

It's **the most comfortable** armchair in the store.

It's **the best** cassette player in the store.

Ordinal Numbers

1st – first
2nd – second
3rd – third
4th – fourth
5th – fifth
•   •
•   •
20th – twentieth
21st – twenty-first
22nd – twenty-second
23rd – twenty-third
24th – twenty-fourth
25th – twenty-fifth
•   •
•   •
•   •
30th – thirtieth

Past Tense

lose–lost
I just **lost** my money.

put–put
What did you **put** in?

Future: Going To

We're **going to** take the kids to the zoo tomorrow.

Should

You **should** ask for your money back.
I think we **should** stop at the bank.
How much do you think we **should** get?

Have To

We **have to** buy stamps.

Time Expressions

We're going to see a movie
on Sunday.
this weekend.
tomorrow.
tomorrow night.
tonight.

Imperatives

Please print your name.

This/That

I like **this** one.
It's larger than **that** one.

Functions and Conversation Strategies in this chapter are listed in the Appendix, pages 202–203.

· EMPLOYMENT/ON THE JOB

15

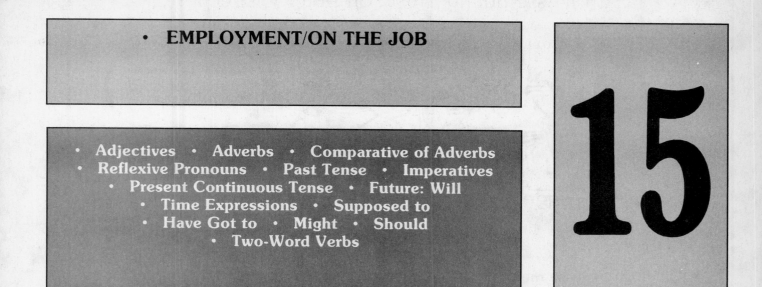

· Adjectives · Adverbs · Comparative of Adverbs · Reflexive Pronouns · Past Tense · Imperatives · Present Continuous Tense · Future: Will · Time Expressions · Supposed to · Have Got to · Might · Should · Two-Word Verbs

Am I Assembling This Computer Correctly?
You Aren't Bagging the Groceries the Right Way
You're a Very Accurate Typist!
Am I Working Fast Enough?
Careful! Put On Your Safety Glasses!
Tony Is Hurt!
Will You Turn Off the Lights When You Leave?
May I Offer a Suggestion?

· Correcting · Approval/Disapproval · Obligation
· Warning · Advice—Suggestions · Complimenting
· Promising · Checking and Indicating Understanding
· Asking for Repetition

Am I Assembling This Computer Correctly?

attach the black wire to the switch on the back

Mr. Johnson

assemble this computer

A. Excuse me.   Mr. Johnson?

B. Yes?

A. Am I assembling this computer correctly?

B. No, not exactly.   You're supposed to attach the black wire to the switch on the back.

A. Oh, I see.   Thank you.

put down the cover

Ms. Andrews

1. use the copying machine

list your hours on this line here

Tracy

2. fill out my timesheet

put the hamburger rolls next to the ketchup

ROLLS

Mr. Hobart

3. stock this shelf

put the forks on the left and the knives and spoons on the right

Mrs. Giovanni

4. set the tables

keep your chest out and your stomach in

Sergeant

5. stand "at attention"

"AM I ASSEMBLING THIS COMPUTER CORRECTLY?"

Now present your own conversations.

You Aren't Bagging the Groceries the Right Way

put the eggs on top

bag the groceries

A. Jimmy?

B. Yes?

A. You aren't bagging the groceries the right way.

B. I'm not?

A. No. You've got to put the eggs on top.

B. Oh. I didn't know that. Thanks for telling me.

load the heaviest boxes first

Mike

1. load the truck

press the white button before you hang up

Elizabeth

2. transfer calls

go back and forth like this

Helen

3. operate the floor polishing machine

say "Room Service" after you knock on the door

Anybody in there? 38

Dennis

4. identify yourself to the guests

smile and say "Welcome to Mr. Chicken!"

MR. CHICKEN   MR. CHICKEN

Brian

5. greet the customers

"YOU AREN'T BAGGING THE GROCERIES THE RIGHT WAY"

Now present your own conversations.

You're a Very Accurate Typist!

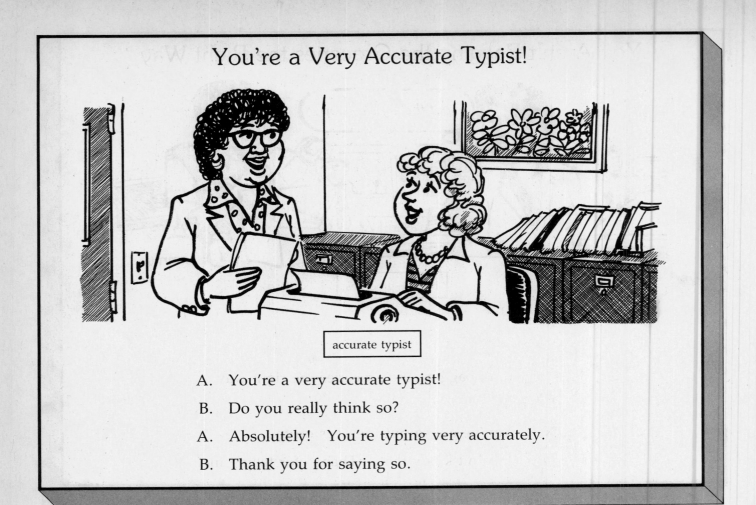

accurate typist

A. You're a very accurate typist!

B. Do you really think so?

A. Absolutely! You're typing very accurately.

B. Thank you for saying so.

1. careful painter

2. neat worker

3. fast* assembler

4. good* actor

5. effective speaker

Now present your own conversations.

* fast–fast
good–well

Am I Working Fast Enough?

work fast	drive carefully
A. Am I working fast enough?	A. Am I driving carefully enough?
B. Actually, you should try to work faster.	B. Actually, you should try to drive more carefully.
A. Oh, okay. I'll try. Thanks for telling me.	A. Oh, okay. I'll try. Thanks for telling me.

1. give the instructions slowly

2. speak to the customers politely

3. make the sandwiches quickly

4. explain this grammar well*

* well–better

5. sing loud

Now present your own conversations.

Careful! Put On Your Safety Glasses!

hurt yourself

A. Careful!

B. Excuse me?

A. Put on your safety glasses! You might hurt yourself.

B. Oh. Thanks for the warning.

1. fall down

2. start a fire

3. get hit by a car

4. get hurt

5. get a shock

Now present your own conversations.

Tony Is Hurt!

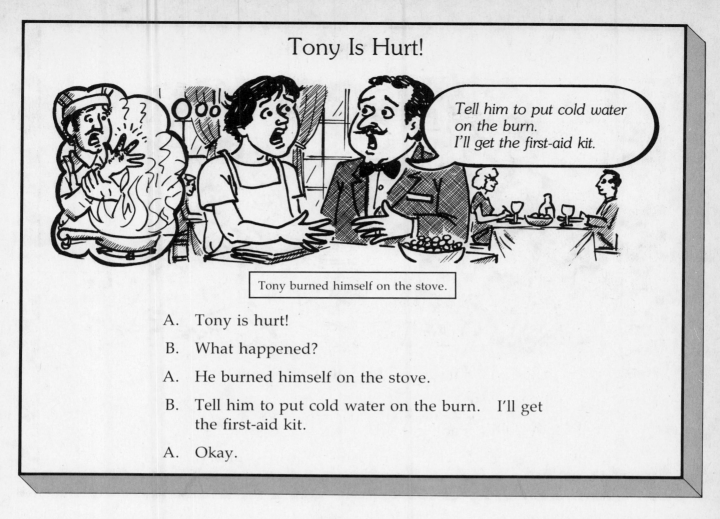

Tell him to put cold water on the burn. I'll get the first-aid kit.

Tony burned himself on the stove.

A. Tony is hurt!

B. What happened?

A. He burned himself on the stove.

B. Tell him to put cold water on the burn. I'll get the first-aid kit.

A. Okay.

Don't move her. I'll call an ambulance.

1. Carol fell* down a flight of stairs.

Turn off the power. I'll call the hospital.

2. Charlie caught* his hand in his machine.

Tell her to press on the cut. I'll call the doctor.

3. Sally cut* herself and she's bleeding VERY badly.

Get her some water. I'll get the school nurse.

4. Mrs. Withers fainted and hit her head on the desk.

Go back and stay with him. I'll call an ambulance.

5. Leo got* hit by a forklift.

"TONY IS HURT"

Now present your own conversations.

* fall–fell   cut–cut
  catch–caught   get–got

Will You Turn Off the Lights When You Leave?

A. Will you turn off the lights when you leave?

B. Yes, I will.

A. Please don't forget.

B. Don't worry.   I promise I'll turn them off.

1. clean up the supply room today

2. mail these packages this afternoon

3. pick up some pencils during your lunch hour

4. type this letter by 4 o'clock

5. put back these "Top Secret" files when you're finished

Now present your own conversations.

INTERCHANGE
May I Offer a Suggestion?

A. Excuse me, Mr. Mitchell.

B. Yes?

A. May I offer a suggestion?

B. Yes.   Please.

A. I think we should put a juice machine with the other vending machines in the employee lounge.

B. I see.   Why do you suggest that?

A. Well, it seems to me that many employees here don't like to drink coffee or soda.

B. Hmm.   You might be right.   Thanks for the suggestion.   I'll think about it.

A. Excuse me, _____.

B. Yes?

A. May I offer a suggestion?

B. Yes.   Please.

A. I think _____.

B. I see.   Why do you suggest that?

A. Well, it seems to me that _____.

B. Hmm.   You might be right.   Thanks for the suggestion.   I'll think about it.

Make a suggestion to your employer using the model dialog above as a guide.   Feel free to adapt and expand the model any way you wish.

Topic Vocabulary

Occupations

actor
assembler
painter
typist
worker

Places on the Job

employee lounge
stairs
supply room

Objects on the Job

box
button
computer
copying machine
desk
files
first-aid kit
floor polishing machine
forklift
forks
fuse box
groceries
knives
letter
lights
machine
package
pencil
shelf
spoons
stove
switch
table
timesheet
truck
vending machine
wire

Job Procedures

assemble *this computer*
attach *the wire*
bag *the groceries*
clean up *the supply room*
drive
explain *this grammar*
fill out *my timesheet*
give *instructions*
go back and forth
greet *the customers*
hang up
identify yourself
knock *on the door*
list *your hours*
load *the truck*
mail *these packages*
make *the sandwiches*
operate *the floor polishing machine*
paint
pick up *some pencils*
press *the button*
put back *these files*
put down *the cover*
put *the hamburger rolls next to the ketchup*
say *"Room Service"*
set *the tables*
smile
speak to *the customers*
stock *this shelf*
transfer *calls*
turn off *the lights*
type *this letter*
use *the copying machine*
work

Feedback on Job Performance

accurate–accurately
careful–carefully
effective–effectively
fast–fast
good–well
loud–loud(ly)
neat–neatly
polite–politely
quick–quickly
slow–slowly

correctly
the right way

Job Safety

Caution
Danger
Do Not Touch
Helmets Required
High Voltage
No Smoking
Wait Here
Warning
Wet Floor

fire
safety glasses

Job Injuries

bleeding
burn *himself*
catch *his hand* in *his* machine
cut *herself*
faint
fall down
get a shock
get hit *by a car*
get hurt
hit *her* head
hurt *yourself*

Job Injury Procedures

Don't move *her.*
Get *her* some water.
Go back and stay with *him.*
Press on the cut.
Put cold water on the burn.
Turn off the power.

Call an ambulance.
Call the doctor.
Call the hospital.
Get *the school nurse.*

Additional Employment Vocabulary

customers
employees
employer
guests
hours
instructions
lunch hour
suggestion

Grammar

Adjectives

You're a very **accurate** typist!

Adverbs

You're typing very **accurately.**
    carefully.
    fast.
    well.

Am I working **fast** enough?

Comparative of Adverbs

You should try to work **slower.**
    faster.

You should try to work **more carefully.**
You should try to speak **more politely.**

You should try to work **better.**

Reflexive Pronouns

He burned **himself.**
She cut **herself.**

Past Tense

catch–caught
He **caught** his hand in his machine.

cut–cut
She **cut** herself.

fall–fell
She **fell** down a flight of stairs.

get–got
He **got** hit by a forklift.

Imperatives

Put on your safety glasses!
Don't smoke in here!

Tell him **to** put cold water on the burn.

Supposed To

You're **supposed to** attach the black wire to the switch.

Time Expressions

Will you mail these packages
by 4 o'clock?
during your lunch hour?
this afternoon?
today?
when you leave?

Have Got To

You've got to put the eggs on top.

Might

You **might** hurt yourself.

Functions and Conversation Strategies in this chapter are listed in the Appendix, pages 203–204.

SCENES & IMPROVISATIONS
Chapters 13, 14, 15

Who do you think these people are?
What do you think they're talking about?
Create conversations based on these scenes and act them out.

1.

2.

3.

4.

5.

6.

7.

8.

16

- **Impersonal Expressions with "You"** • **Past Tense**
  • **Past Continuous Tense** • **Future: Going to**
• **Future: Will** • **Have to** • **Should** • **Ought to**

Are You Allowed to Swim Here?
You Aren't Allowed to Park Here
"No Right Turn on Red"
Let Me See Your License
Rules of the Building
When Are You Going to Fix My Sink?
Do I Have to Work on July 4th?
You Should Write to the Mayor

• Permission • Asking for and Reporting Information
• Surprise–Disbelief • Promising • Focusing Attention
• Checking and Indicating Understanding • Initiating a Topic

Are You Allowed to Swim Here?

A. Are you allowed to swim here?

B. Yes, you are.

A. Thanks.

A. Are you allowed to smoke here?

B. No, you aren't.

A. Oh, okay. Thanks.

1.

2.

3.

4.

5.

Now present your own conversations.

You Aren't Allowed to Park Here

A. Excuse me. You aren't allowed to park here.

B. Oh?

A. Yes. There's the sign.

B. Hmm. "Parking for Handicapped Only." I didn't see the sign. Thanks for telling me.

A. You're welcome.

1. smoke

2. walk

3. stand

4. come in

5. eat

Now present your own conversations.

"No Right Turn on Red"

A. Oh, my goodness!*

B. What's the matter?

A. Didn't you see the sign?

B. The sign? No. What did it say?

A. "No Right Turn on Red."

B. "No Right Turn on Red"?!

A. Yes.

B. Oh, my goodness!*

1.

2.

3.

4.

5.

Now present your own conversations.

* Oh, my goodness!
  Oops!
  Uh-oh!

164

Let Me See Your License

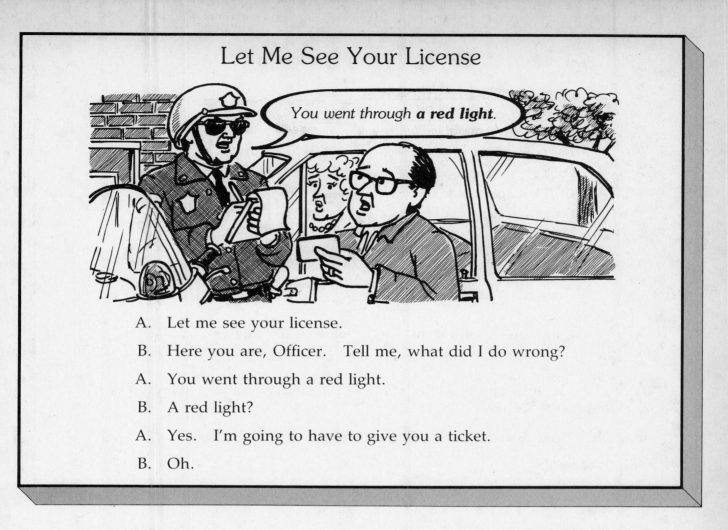

A. Let me see your license.

B. Here you are, Officer.   Tell me, what did I do wrong?

A. You went through a red light.

B. A red light?

A. Yes.   I'm going to have to give you a ticket.

B. Oh.

1.

2.

3.

4.

5.

Now present your own conversations.

Rules of the Building

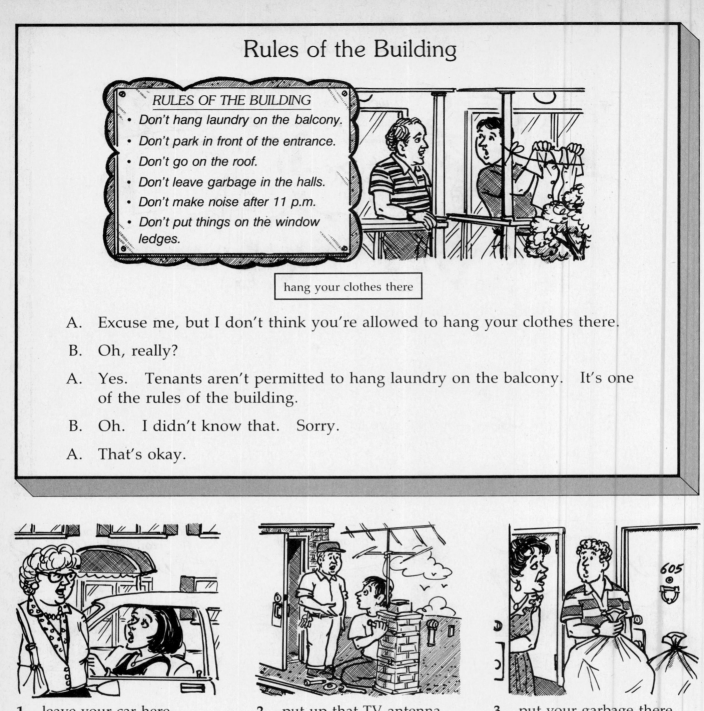

RULES OF THE BUILDING
- *Don't hang laundry on the balcony.*
- *Don't park in front of the entrance.*
- *Don't go on the roof.*
- *Don't leave garbage in the halls.*
- *Don't make noise after 11 p.m.*
- *Don't put things on the window ledges.*

hang your clothes there

A. Excuse me, but I don't think you're allowed to hang your clothes there.

B. Oh, really?

A. Yes. Tenants aren't permitted to hang laundry on the balcony. It's one of the rules of the building.

B. Oh. I didn't know that. Sorry.

A. That's okay.

1. leave your car here

2. put up that TV antenna

3. put your garbage there

4. play your stereo so loud at this hour

5. put flowerpots there

"RULES OF THE BUILDING"

Now present your own conversations.

When Are You Going to Fix My Sink?

Mr. Grant in Apartment 2

A. Hello. This is Mr. Grant in Apartment 2.

B. Yes? What can I do for you?

A. I'm wondering . . . When are you going to fix my sink?

B. Well, Mr. Grant, I'm very busy right now. I'll try to fix it soon.

A. You know, you promised to fix it several weeks ago. I'm afraid I'm going to have to call the Health Department.

B. Now, Mr. Grant. I'm sure that won't be necessary. I promise I'll fix your sink this week.

A. Thank you very much.

1. Mrs. Lee in Apartment 9F

2. Bill Franklin in Building 4

3. Anita Davis, who lived in Apartment 6D

4. Ms. Fernandez at 659 Central Avenue

5. Mr. Dempsey on the fifth floor

Now present your own conversations.

Do I Have to Work on July 4th?

A. May I ask you a question?

B. Sure.   What is it?

A. Do I have to work on July 4th?

B. No, you don't.   It's a legal holiday.

A. I see.   Thank you.

1.

2.

3.

4.

5.

Now present your own conversations.

INTERCHANGE
You Should Write to the Mayor

A. You know . . . in my opinion, they should have more buses on this route in the morning.

B. Why do you say that?

A. The lines at the bus stops are long, the buses are too crowded, and people are often late for work.

B. Hmm. You should write to the mayor.*

A. Write to the mayor?

B. Yes. Really. You ought to write to the mayor and express your opinion.

A. That's a good idea. I will.

* **Some Forms of Citizen Participation**
  write to/call the President
  write to/call our congressman/congresswoman/senator
  write to/call the governor/mayor/city manager
  speak at a town meeting
  send a letter to the newspaper
  call a radio talk show

A. You know . . . in my opinion, _____.

B. Why do you say that?

A. _____, _____, and _____.

B. Hmm. You should _____.*

A. _____?

B. Yes. Really. You ought to _____ and express your opinion.

A. That's a good idea. I will.

You're talking with a friend about a local, national, or international issue. Create an original conversation using the model dialog above as a guide. Feel free to adapt and expand the model any way you wish.

Topic Vocabulary

Housing

apartment
balcony
building
entrance
garbage
hall
heat
kitchen
laundry
lead paint
noise
roof
rules
security deposit
tenant
TV antenna
window ledge

Recreation

camp
fish
ice skate
play ball
swim

Signs

Do Not Enter
Keep Off the Grass
No Fishing
No Food or Drinks
No Parking
No Smoking
No Standing in Front of the
    White Line
Parking for Handicapped Only

Road Signs

Do Not Enter
No Left Turn
No Right Turn on Red
No U Turn
One Way
Stop

Driving

illegal
license
90 miles per hour
Officer
red light
road
stop sign
ticket
U turn
wrong side of the road

drive
drive through *a stop sign*
go *90* miles per hour
go through *a red light*
make *an illegal U* turn
speed

Household Repairs

fix *my sink*
remove *the lead paint*
repair *our toilet*
spray *our apartment*
turn on *our heat*

Employee Rights

legal holiday
lunch break
maternity leave
overtime
radioactive
safety rules
union rules

Tenants' Rights

Channel 7 News
City Hall
court
Health Department
Housing Authority

Citizen Participation

call
express *your* opinion
send a letter
speak
write to

city manager
congressman
congresswoman
governor
mayor
President
senator

newspaper
radio talk show
town meeting

Grammar

Impersonal Expressions with "You"

Are **you** allowed to swim here?
    Yes, **you** are.
    No, **you** aren't.

You aren't allowed to park here.
I don't think **you're** allowed to
    hang your clothes there.

Past Tense

What **did** I do wrong?
    You **went** through a red light.

Past Continuous Tense

You **were** speed**ing**.
You **were** driv**ing** on the wrong
    side of the road.

Future: Going To

When are you **going to** fix my
    sink?

I'm **going to** have to call the
    Health Department.

Future: Will

I'**ll** try to fix it soon.
I promise I'**ll** fix your sink this
    week.

I'm sure that **won't** be necessary.

Have To

Do I **have to** work on July 4th?

Should

They **should** have more buses
    on this route.
You **should** write to the mayor.

Ought To

You **ought to** write to the mayor.

Functions and Conversation Strategies in this chapter are listed in the Appendix, **page 204.**

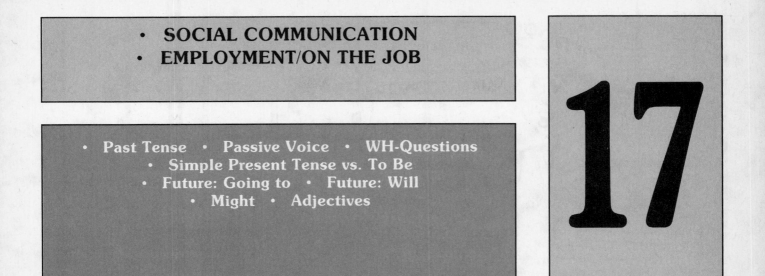

SOCIAL COMMUNICATION
EMPLOYMENT/ON THE JOB

17

- Past Tense • Passive Voice • WH-Questions
- Simple Present Tense vs. To Be
- Future: Going to • Future: Will
- Might • Adjectives

I'm Sorry to Interrupt
What Does That Mean?
What's New with You?
Did You Hear the News?
I Like Your New Car
Did You See the "Phil Crosby Show" Last Night?
Did You Do Anything Special Over the Weekend?
What Are You Going to Do on Your Next Day Off?

- Asking for and Reporting Information • Complimenting
- Satisfaction/Dissatisfaction • Congratulating • Sympathizing
- Checking and Indicating Understanding • Initiating a Topic
- Interrupting • Clarification

I'm Sorry to Interrupt

A. Excuse me. I'm sorry to interrupt, but we're out of fries.
B. Did you say pies?
A. No. Fries.
B. Oh, okay. Thank you.

Now present your own conversations.

What Does That Mean?

A. Our computers are down.

B. I'm afraid I'm not following you. What does that mean?

A. What that means is they aren't working right now.

B. Oh. I understand.

1. "There aren't any more seats on the plane."

2. "You're in excellent health."

3. "I'll pay for the dinner."

4. "He quit*."

5. "It's very popular."

Now present your own conversations.

* throw–threw
quit–quit

What's New with You?

My son just got engaged.

A. What's new with you?
B. Nothing much. How about you?
A. I have some good news.
B. Really? What?
A. My son just got engaged.
B. That's great! Congratulations!

I lost my wallet yesterday.

A. What's new with you?
B. Nothing much. How about you?
A. I have some bad news.
B. Really? What?
A. I lost my wallet yesterday.
B. That's too bad! I'm sorry to hear that.

1. I just received a raise.

2. My husband got fired from his job.

3. I'm going to be promoted.

4. Our landlord is going to raise our rent again next month.

5. My daughter had a baby boy yesterday.

Now present your own conversations.

174

Did You Hear the News?

The boss is going to retire.

I heard it in the cafeteria.

A. Did you hear the news?

B. No. What?

A. The boss is going to retire.

B. Really? I can't believe it! Where did you hear that?

A. I heard it in the cafeteria.

B. Well, I'm really surprised.

They might lay off the workers on the night shift.

1. I heard it in the employee lounge.

Our supervisor had a big argument with the boss.

2. One of the secretaries told* me.

We might go on strike.

3. They talked about it at a union meeting.

The company is going to transfer Mr. Kendall to the West Coast office.

4. I overheard* it on the elevator.

The office manager and the receptionist got married last weekend.

5. Everybody in the office is talking about it.

"DID YOU HEAR THE NEWS?"

Now present your own conversations.

* tell–told   overhear–overheard

175

I Like Your New Car

A. I like your new car. It's very fancy.
B. Thank you.
A. How does it ride?
B. Very well.

1. engagement ring
beautiful

2. jeans
stylish

3. daughter
friendly

4. haircut
nice

5. new coat
attractive

Now present your own conversations.

* buy–bought

Did You See the "Phil Crosby Show" Last Night?

A. Did you see the "Phil Crosby Show" last night?

B. No, I didn't.

A. You missed a really good one.

B. Oh? What happened?

A. Phil went to the zoo with his children and a monkey stole* his wallet.

B. Oh. Was it funny?

A. Yes. It was VERY funny.

B. I'm sorry I missed it.

Phil went to the zoo with his children and a monkey stole his wallet.

1. Dr. Crane fell in love with one of his patients.

2. They interviewed the President.

3. Monica hit Molly's boyfriend with a lamp.

4. Hernandez hit five home runs.

5. Green people from Mars attacked San Francisco.

Now present your own conversations.

* steal–stole

Did You Do Anything Special Over the Weekend?

go to a rock concert

A. Did you do anything special over the weekend?

B. Yes.   I went to a rock concert.

A. Oh.   Who did you go with?

B. I went with my boyfriend.

A. Did you enjoy it?

B. Yes.   We enjoyed it a lot.

1. go skiing with my family

2. see a movie

3. go to a ballgame

4. go to the Super Bowl

5. take my children to New York City

Now present your own conversations.

What Are You Going to Do on Your Next Day Off?

 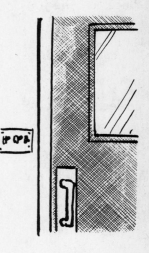

A. What are you going to do on your next day off?

B. I'm not sure.   I'll probably clean my apartment.   How about you?

A. I don't know.   I might go to a museum, or maybe I'll visit my parents. I'm not sure yet.

B. Well, whatever you decide to do, I hope you enjoy yourself.

A. Thanks.   You, too.

A. What are you going to do _____?

B. I'm not sure.   I'll probably _____.   How about you?

A. I don't know.   I might _____, or maybe I'll _____. I'm not sure yet.

B. Well, whatever you decide to do, I hope you enjoy yourself.

A. Thanks.   You, too.

You and a co-worker are talking about your plans.   Create an original conversation using the model dialog above as a guide.   Feel free to adapt and expand the model any way you wish.

Topic Vocabulary

Places on the Job

cafeteria
elevator
employee lounge
fifth floor
Room *15*

Objects on the Job

nails
phone
screws

People on the Job

boss
co-worker
office manager
receptionist
secretary
supervisor
workers

Additional Employment Vocabulary

company
night shift
office
strike
union meeting

be promoted
get fired
lay off
quit
raise
retire
transfer

day off
holiday
vacation
weekend

Describing

attractive
beautiful
fancy
friendly
nice
stylish

dramatic
exciting
funny
interesting
scary

Recreation and Entertainment

ballgame
Broadway show
game
movie
mountain
museum
rock concert
show
Super Bowl
tickets

Grammar

Past Tense

Did you hear the news?
Where **did** you hear that?
No, I **didn't.**

Was it funny?
  It **was** very funny.

Dr. Crane **fell** in love.
My husband **got** fired from his job.
My daughter **had** a baby boy yesterday.
I **heard** it in the employee lounge.
Monica **hit** Molly's boyfriend.
I **lost** my wallet yesterday.
I **saw** "Star Battles."
Phil **went** to the zoo.

      buy–bought
I **bought** them at Sears.

      overhear–overheard
I **overheard** it on the elevator.

      quit–quit
He **quit.**

      steal–stole
A monkey **stole** his wallet.

      tell–told
One of the secretaries **told** me.

      throw–threw
Mr. Haskins **threw** in the towel today.

Passive Voice

My son just **got engaged.**
My husband **got fired** from his job.
I'm going to **be promoted.**

WH-Questions

Who cut it?
What is her name?
When did you get it?
Where did you buy them?
Why are you wearing it?
Which game did you see?
How does it ride?

Simple Present Tense vs. To Be

We need some more nails.
Tim Ross wants to see you.

Mrs. Hall **is** on the phone.
We're out of fries.
There's a broken window on the fifth floor.

Future: Will

I'll probably clean my apartment.
Maybe I'll visit my parents.

Future: Going To

I'm **going to** be promoted.
Our landlord is **going to** raise our rent.

What are you **going to** do on your next day off?

Might

I **might** go to a museum.
We **might** go on strike.
They **might** lay off the workers on the night shift.

Adjectives

It's very **fancy.**

Was it **funny?**
  It was very **funny.**

Functions and Conversation Strategies in this chapter are listed in the Appendix, page 205.

• Should • Short Answers • Pronoun Review
• Have Got to • Have to • Time Expressions
• Possessive Nouns

How Is David Doing in Math This Year?
This Is Mrs. Smith, the School Principal, Calling
I Agree
I Disagree
I've Really Got to Go Now
So Long
In My Opinion

• Agreement/Disagreement • Leave Taking • Obligation
• Asking for and Reporting Information • Initiating a Topic
• Focusing Attention

How Is David Doing in Math This Year?

Mrs. Carter
David

A. Hello. I'm Mrs. Carter.

B. Oh! David's mother! I'm pleased to meet you.

A. Nice to meet you, too. Tell me, how is David doing in Math this year?

B. He's doing very well. He works very hard, and his grades are excellent. You should be very proud of him.

A. I'm happy to hear that. Thank you.

1. Mr. Taylor
Judy

2. Mrs. Lee
George

3. Mr. and Mrs. Williams
Beth

4. Mrs. Mitchell
Tommy and Timmy

5. Mr. Atlas
Jack

Now present your own conversations.

This Is Mrs. Smith, the School Principal, Calling

A. Hello?

B. Hello. Is this Mr. Johnson?

A. Yes, it is.

B. This is Mrs. Smith, the school principal, calling.

A. Yes?

B. Michael started a fight in the school cafeteria this morning.

A. He did?

B. I'm afraid he did.

A. All right. I promise I'll speak to him about this when he gets home. Thank you for letting me know.

B. You're welcome. Good-bye.

Michael started a fight in the school cafeteria this morning.

Mr. Johnson

Mrs. Smith, the school principal

Wendy isn't doing her History homework.

Mrs. Thomas

Mr. Baker, Wendy's History teacher

1.

Richard didn't come for his eye test today.

Mrs. Lane

Miss Fenwick, the school nurse

2.

Patty is cutting classes every day.

Ms. Wilkins

Mr. Harris, Patty's guidance counselor

3.

Diane came to school late every day this week.

Mr. Robertson

Ms. Pepper, Diane's homeroom teacher

4.

Henry won't take a shower after gym class.

Mr. Simmons

Coach Bradley

5.

"THIS IS MRS. SMITH, THE SCHOOL PRINCIPAL, CALLING"

Now present your own conversations.

183

I Agree

The boss is in a terrible mood today.

We probably shouldn't bother him.

A. You know . . . the boss is in a terrible mood today.

B. I agree. He is.

A. We probably shouldn't bother him.

B. You're right. I was thinking the same thing.

These copies don't look very good.

Maybe we should do them again.

1.

The soup is cold.

It doesn't taste very good.

2.

The mall was very quiet today.

Everybody was probably at the beach.

3.

Our English teacher taught us a lot.

We should have a party for her.

LAST CLASS TODAY

4.

It looks like a storm is coming.

We should probably close the pool.

5.

"I AGREE"

Now present your own conversations.

I Disagree

A. You know . . . I think this bread is stale.

B. Oh? Why do you say that?

A. It feels very hard. Don't you agree?

B. No, not really. I disagree.

1.

2.

3.

4.

5.

Now present your own conversations.

I've Really Got to Go Now

get back to work

A. By the way, what time is it?

B. It's 1:30.

A. Oh! It's late! I've really got to go now. I have to get back to work.

B. Okay. See you soon.

A. Good-bye.

1. pick up my kids at school

2. get to class

3. mail these letters before the post office closes

4. get to the bank by 4:00

5. be at the White House in ten minutes

Now present your own conversations.

So Long

pick up my wife at the office

A. You know, I think I should be going now. I've got to pick up my wife at the office.

B. I should be going, too.

A. So long.

B. See you soon.

1. be home before dark

2. buy some food for dinner

3. catch the 6:23 train

4. meet with my advisor in five minutes

5. get to my next performance

Now present your own conversations.

INTERCHANGE
In My Opinion

A. You know . . . I think English is an easy language to learn.   Don't you agree?

B. Well, I'm not so sure.   Why do you say that?

A. The grammar rules are very easy.   Don't you think so?

B. No, not really.   I disagree.   In my opinion, English is a very difficult language.

A. Oh?   What makes you say that?

B. You don't always pronounce English words the way you spell them.

A. Hmm.   Maybe you're right.

A. You know . . . I think _____.
Don't you agree?

B. Well, I'm not so sure.   Why do you say that?

A. _____. Don't you think so?

B. No, not really.   I disagree.   In my opinion, _____
_____.

A. Oh?   What makes you say that?

B. _____.

A. Hmm.   Maybe you're right.

You're having a disagreement with somebody. Create an original conversation using the model dialog on p. 188 as a guide. Feel free to adapt and expand the model any way you wish.

Topic Vocabulary

School Subjects

French
History
Math
Physical Education (gym class)
Science
Spelling

School Personnel

advisor
coach
guidance counselor
homeroom teacher
nurse
principal
teacher

Additional Education Vocabulary

cafeteria
class
eye test
grades
homework

Employment

boss
classified ads
copy
job
office
office assistant
supervisor

Grammar

Should

I think I **should** be going now.
Maybe we **should** do them again.

We probably **shouldn't** bother him.

Short Answers

It does.
They don't.
He is.
She is.
It is.
She isn't.
He did.
She did.
He didn't.
It was.
He won't.

Pronoun Review

He works very hard.
His grades are excellent.
You should be very proud of **him**.

She works very hard.
Her grades are excellent.
You should be very proud of **her**.

They work very hard.
Their grades are excellent.
You should be very proud of **them**.

Have Got To

I've got to go now.
I've got to pick up my wife at the office.

Have To

I **have to** get back to work.

Time Expressions

It's **3:00 (three o'clock)**.
It's **1:30 (one thirty)**.
It's **11:20 (eleven twenty)**.
It's **4:45 (four forty-five)**.

I have to mail these letters
before the post office closes.
by 4:00.
in ten **minutes**.

Possessive Nouns

/s/   Jack's father
/z/   David's mother
/ɪz/   George's mother

Functions and Conversation Strategies in this chapter are listed in the Appendix, pages 205–206.

SCENES & IMPROVISATIONS
Chapters 16, 17, 18

Who do you think these people are?
What do you think they're talking about?
Create conversations based on these scenes and act them out.

1.

2.

3.

4.

5.

6.

7.

8.

CHAPTER-BY-CHAPTER SUMMARY OF FUNCTIONS AND CONVERSATION STRATEGIES

CHAPTER 1

Functions

Greeting People

Hello.
Hi. [less formal]

Nice to meet you.
   Nice meeting you, too.

How are you?
   Fine.
   Fine, thanks.

Introductions

Introducing Oneself

My name is *Carlos*.
I'm *Kim*.

Introducing Others

I'd like to introduce you to *my husband,
Michael*.

Asking for and Reporting Information

What's your name?
What's your last name?
And your first name?

Could you spell that, please?
S-A-N-C-H-E-Z.

What's your address?
10 Main Street.
And your telephone number?
423-6978.

Where are you from?
New York.
I'm from *New York*.

Are you from *Tokyo*?

Are you *American*?

How about you?
And you?

CHAPTER 2

Functions

Asking for and Reporting Information

What city?
   Chicago.
What street?
   Hudson Avenue.

How do you spell that?
   N-I-E-L-S-O-N.

The number is *863-4227*.

Is this *328-7178*?

Is *Peter* there?
   No, *he* isn't. *He's at the supermarket*.

Where are you going?
   To *the library*.
   I'm going to *the library*.

And you?
How about you?

What are you doing?
   I'm *fixing my car*.

Greeting People

Hello.
Hi. [less formal]

Hello, *Fred?*
Hello. This is *Mike*.
Hello, *Steve?* This is *Jackie*.

How are you today?
How are you doing? [less formal]
   Fine.
   Fine, thanks.
   Pretty good.

Identifying

Hello. This is *Mike*.

Leave Taking

Nice seeing you.
   Nice seeing you, too.

I'll call back later.

Speak to you soon.

Good-bye.

Apologizing

I'm sorry.
Sorry.

Gratitude

Expressing. . .

Thank you.

CHAPTER 3

Functions

Directions-Location

Asking for Directions

Can you tell me how to get to
_____?
Can you please tell me how to get to
_____?
Can you possibly tell me how to get to
_____?

Giving Directions

Walk THAT way.

Turn right.
Turn left.

Walk that way to *Second Avenue* and
   turn *right*.

Go *two* blocks to *Grove Street*.

Turn *left* on *Grove Street*.
Turn *right* at *Grand Avenue*.

Look for the *museum* on the *right*.

Take *the Second Avenue bus* and get off
   at *Park Street*.
Take *the West Side Expressway* and get
   off at *Exit 14*.

Drive that way *two* miles.

Inquiring about Location

Is there a *post office* nearby?

Giving Location

There's a *post office* on *Main Street*.
It's on *Main Street*.
It's on *Main Street, next to the bank*.

It's

$$\left\{\begin{array}{l}\text{next to}\\\text{across from}\\\text{around the corner}\\\text{from}\end{array}\right\}\text{the bank.}$$

It's between *the library* and *the clinic*.

The *bus station* is $\left\{\begin{array}{l}\text{on the left.}\\\text{on the right.}\end{array}\right.$

The *bus station* is on the *left, next to the post office*.

Asking for and Reporting Information

Does this *bus* go to *Westville?*
  It goes to *Riverside*.

Which *bus* goes to *Westville?*
  The Number 30 bus.

Is this *Bus Number 42?*
Is this the *plane* to *Atlanta?*
Does this *bus* stop *at Center Street?*
Does this *plane* go to *Florida?*

Where do I *get off?*
  At *Park Street*.

Attracting Attention

Excuse me.

Gratitude

Expressing . . .

Thank you.
Thank you very much.
Thanks.
Thanks very much.

Conversation Strategies

Checking and Indicating Understanding

Checking Another Person's Understanding

Okay so far?

Have you got that?

Checking One's Own Understanding

On Main Street?

I'm sorry. Did you say *the Second Avenue bus?*

Indicating Understanding

Okay.

Uh-húh.

I see.

I understand.

I'm following you.

Asking for Repetition

I'm sorry. Could you please repeat that?

WHERE *do I get off?*

CHAPTER 4

Functions

Asking for and Reporting Information

Can you describe it?

Is there *a refrigerator in the kitchen?*

How many *windows* are there?

There's *a very nice refrigerator in the kitchen*.
There are *four windows in the living room*.

How much is *the rent?*
  It's *$700 a month*.
Does that include *utilities?*
  It includes *everything except electricity*.

There isn't any more *milk*.
There aren't any more *cookies*.

What's in it?
What's in them?

Want-Desire

Inquiring about . . .

Do you want to *see the apartment?*

Where do you want *this sofa?*

Expressing . . .

We're looking for *a two-bedroom apartment*.

Directions-Location

Inquiring about Location

Where's *the butter?*
Where are *the carrots?*

Giving Location

It's in Aisle 3.
They're in Aisle *J*.

Describing

It has *two bedrooms*.

Instructing

Put it *in the living room*.
Please put it *in the living room*.

Surprise-Disbelief

There isn't?
There aren't?

Attracting Attention

Excuse me.

Correcting

Giving Correction

No. *"J."*

Gratitude

Thank you.
Thanks.

Complimenting

Expressing Compliments

Mmm!

This *cake* is delicious!
These *egg rolls* are delicious!

It's excellent!
They're excellent!

Responding to Compliments

I'm glad you like it.
I'm glad you like them.

Thank you for saying so.

Conversation Strategies

Hesitating

Hmm.
Let me see.
Let me think . . .

Checking and Indicating Understanding

Checking One's Own Understanding

$700 a month plus electricity?

I'm sorry. Did you say *"A?"*

CHAPTER 5

Functions

Asking for and Reporting Information

What's your name?
  Ann Kramer.

Tell me about *your skills.*
Can you tell me about *the work schedule?*

What do you want to know?

What job do you have open?

Is that job still open?

Are you currently employed?
  Yes, I am. I work at *Tyler's Department Store.*
  No, not at the moment. My last job was at *the Seven Seas Restaurant.*

What is your position there?
  I'm a *salesperson.*
What was your position there?
  I was a *waiter.*

How long have you worked there?
How long did you work there?
  Three years.

What are the job responsibilities of a *stock clerk* here?
  A stock clerk stocks the shelves.

I *stock the shelves* in my present job.

Hours are *from nine to five thirty.*
The salary is *five dollars an hour.*

I'm *married.*

My *husband's* name is *Richard.*
He's a security guard at the National Motors factory.

We have *two* children, *a son and a daughter.*

Where are you originally from?
  I'm from *Dallas.*

Do you have any hobbies or special interests?
  I *play the piano.*

Asking for and Reporting Additional Information

Do you have any other questions?

Tell me a little more about *yourself.*
Can you tell me a little more about *the position?*

And may I ask *about the salary?*

Ability/Inability

Inquiring about . . .

Can you *make eggs and sandwiches?*
Can you *come in on Monday at 10:00?*

Do you know how to *take inventory?*

Do you think you can *do that?*

Expressing Ability

Yes.
Yes, I can.

I can *use a cash register.*
I can *take inventory* very well.

I know how to *talk with customers.*

Expressing Inability

No, I can't.

Certainty/Uncertainty

Inquiring about . . .

Are you sure?

Expressing Certainty

I'm sure *I can learn quickly.*
I know *I can learn very quickly.*

I'm positive.

Yes, definitely!

Requests

Direct, Polite

Can I *talk to the manager?*

Want-Desire

Expressing . . .

We're looking for *a cook.*

I'd like to *apply.*

Gratitude

Expressing . . .

Thank you.
Thank you very much.
Thanks very much.

Responding to . . .

My pleasure.

Appreciation

I appreciate *the time you've taken to talk with me.*

Conversation Strategies

Checking and Indicating Understanding

Checking One's Own Understanding

On Monday at 10:00?

Indicating Understanding

I understand.
I see.

Hesitating

Let's see . . .

CHAPTER 6

Functions

Asking for and Reporting Information

Are you feeling okay?
  No, not really.

What's the matter?
What's the problem?
  I have *a headache.*
  My *right foot* hurts very badly.
  My *neck* is very *stiff.*
  He's feeling very *dizzy.*
  She has a bad *toothache.*
  My *ears* are *ringing.*

My *father* is *having a heart attack!*
My *wife* can't *breathe!*
My *son* is *bleeding* very badly!
My apartment is on fire!
There's a *burglar in my house!*

Do you *smoke?*
Are you *allergic to penicillin?*
Is there a history of *heart disease* in your family?
Do you have *any allergies?*
Are you currently *taking any medication?*

I want to report an emergency!

What's your name?
  Diane Perkins.
And the address?
  76 Lake Street.
Telephone number?
  293-7637.

Instructing

Touch *your toes.*
Take off *your shirt.*
Sit *on the table.*
Hold *your breath.*
Lie *on your back.*
Look *at the ceiling.*
Say "a-a-h"!

Be sure to *follow the directions on the label.*

Take *one tablet three times* a day.
Take *two tablets* before *each meal.*
Take *two capsules* after *each meal.*

Advice-Suggestions

Asking for . . .

What do you recommend?

Offering . . .

I recommend *Maxi-Fed Cold Medicine.*

You should *go on a diet.*

I suggest that you *lose 15 pounds.*

Responding to . . .

Thank you for the advice.

Directions-Location

Inquiring about Location

Where can I find *it?*
Where can I find *them?*

Giving Location

It's in Aisle 2 {
  on the right.
  on the left.
  on the top shelf.
  on the middle shelf.
  on the bottom shelf.
}
It's in the back near *the aspirin.*
It's in the front near the *cash register.*

Sympathizing

I'm sorry to hear that.

Attracting Attention

Excuse me.

Requests

Direct, Polite

Can you help me?

196

Gratitude

Expressing . . .

Thank you.
Thanks.

Identifying

Doctor's Office.
Police.
City Hospital.
Jones Ambulance Company.
Fire Department.
Police Emergency Unit.

Want-Desire

Inquiring about . . .

Do you want to *make an appointment?*

Ability/Inability

Inquiring about . . .

Can you *come in tomorrow morning?*

Asking for and Reporting Additional Information

I have just one more question.

Fear-Worry-Anxiety

I'm concerned about *your weight.*

Conversation Strategies

Checking and Indicating Understanding

Checking One's Own Understanding

Maxi-Fed Cold Medicine?
Tomorrow morning at 9:15?
My toes?
My weight?

One tablet three times a day.

Indicating Understanding

I see.
I understand.

Initiating a Topic

You know . . .

CHAPTER 7

Functions

Want-Desire

Inquiring about . . .

What *size do you want?*

Do you want to *try on another one?*

How do you want to *send it?*

Expressing . . .

I'm looking for *a shirt.*

I'd like to *buy this watch.*
I want to *return this fan.*
I want to *buy some stamps,* please.

I'd like *a refund,* please.

Directions-Location

Inquiring about Location

Where are *the rest rooms?*

Giving Location

Shirts are {
  in Aisle 3.
  over there.
  on that *counter.*
  in the back of *the store.*
  in the front of *the store.*
  on the *fourth* floor.
  near *the elevator.*
  in *the basement.*
}

Satisfaction/Dissatisfaction

Inquiring about . . .

How *does the jacket fit?*

Expressing Dissatisfaction

It's too *short.*
They're too *long.*

Attracting Attention

Excuse me.

Gratitude

Expressing . . .

Thank you.
Thank you very much.
Thanks.
Thanks very much.

Requests

Direct, Polite

Can you *help me?*

Please *insure it for fifty dollars.*

Responding to Requests

Certainly.
All right.

Offering to Help

Making an Offer

May I help you?

Responding to an Offer

Yes, please.

Asking for and Reporting Information

That's *twenty-six ninety-five.*
That comes to *twenty-six ninety-five.*

It's *ten percent* off.
They're *half price.*

What's the matter with *it?*

Where's it going?
  To *Detroit.*

Is it *valuable?*
  Yes, it is. It's a *camera.*

Correcting

Giving Correction

Excuse me, but I don't think *that's the right price.*

You're *at* the wrong *window.*

Responding to Correction

Oh. You're right.

Apologizing

I'm sorry.
I apologize.

Granting Forgiveness

That's okay.

Conversation Strategies

Checking and Indicating Understanding

Checking One's Own Understanding

Okay. Let's see . . . *a size 36 black belt.*

The fourth floor?
Window Number 2?

Hesitating

Hmm.

CHAPTER 8

Functions

Requests

Direct, Polite

Please *take this box to Mr. Miller.*

Can you *show me how to turn on this machine?*

Could you *tell me how to transfer a call?*

Direct, More Polite

Can you help me for a minute?
Could you help me for a minute?

Could you possibly show me how?

Responding to Requests

Yes.
Sure.
Certainly.
All right.

Instructing

Press *this button.*
Pull *this chain.*
Push *this button.*
Flip *this switch.*

Put in your time card like this.

First, *take out your tray.*
Then, *close the drawer.*

Attracting Attention

Excuse me.

Johnson?

Approval/Disapproval

Inquiring about . . .

Did I *wash the glasses* all right?

Expressing Approval

You *washed them* very well.

Expressing Disapproval

You *typed them* rather poorly.

Apologizing

I'm sorry.

I'm sorry, but *I'm new here.*

Directions-Location

Inquiring about Location

Where's *the supply room?*

Giving Location

It's down the hall.
It's down the hall on the *left.*
It's in the *basement.*
It's the *first* door on the *right.*

Gratitude

Expressing . . .

Thank you.
Thanks.
Thank you very much.
Thanks very much.

Responding to . . .

You're welcome.

Introductions

Introducing Oneself

My name is *Bill.*
I'm *Patty.*

Greeting People

Welcome to *the company.*

Asking for and Reporting Information

What does he look like?

How's *your first day on the job going?*
  Fine.

Tell me, _____?

What did I do wrong?

Where's *your helmet?*

Describing

He's *tall*, with *brown* hair.

Ability/Inability

Inquiring about . . .

Do you know how to *lock the cash register*?

Expressing Inability

No, I don't.

Correcting

Giving Correction

Actually, *you didn't*.

You *made several spelling mistakes*.

Granting Forgiveness

Don't worry about it.

Denying/Admitting

Admitting

I'm afraid *I left it in my car*.

Remembering/Forgetting

Indicating . . .

I forgot.

Offering to Help

Making an Offer

I'm free now. What do you want me to do?

Is there anything else I can do?

Do you want me to *set the tables*?

Complimenting

Expressing Compliments

You're an excellent *employee*.

Responding to Compliments

Thank you for saying so.

Obligation

Expressing . . .

You're required to *wear your helmet at all times*.

Conversation Strategies

Checking and Indicating Understanding

Checking Another Person's Understanding

Okay so far?

Have you got that?

Checking One's Own Understanding

To Mr. Miller?

First, *I press the button*. Then, *I dial the office*. Right?

Indicating Understanding

I see.

Yes. That's right.

Um-hḿm.

I'm following you.
I understand.

Asking for Repetition

I'm sorry. Could you please repeat that?

Hesitating

Uh . . .

Focusing Attention

You know, *you're required to wear your helmet*.

CHAPTER 9

Functions

Want-Desire

Inquiring about . . .

What do you want to do?
What do you want to do today?

Do you want to *see a movie*?

Expressing . . .

I want to *go jogging*.

I don't want to *play tennis*.

Asking for and Reporting Information

Tell me, _____?

What's the weather like?
   It's *raining*.

What's the weather forecast?
   It's going to *be hot*.

I heard in *on the radio*.
I heard it *on the 7 o'clock news*.
I read it *in the paper*.
I saw *the forecast* on TV.
I called *the Weather Information number*.

How was *your weekend*?
   It was *very nice*.
What did you do?
   I *went skiing*.

Did you *do anything special*?

I was at *the movies*.

What *movie* did you *see*?
Who did you *hear*?

Invitations

Extending . . .

Do you want to *get together tomorrow*?

Accepting . . .

Sure.

That sounds like fun.

Declining . . .

I'm afraid I can't.

Maybe we can *go out for dinner* some other time.

Likes/Dislikes

Inquiring about . . .

What do you like to do in your free time?

Do you like to *run*?

Where do you like to *run*?
What do you like to *bake*?
What kind of *books* do you like to *read*?
Which *program* do you like?

Who's your favorite *movie star*?

Expressing Likes

I like to *run*.
I like to *run* a lot.

I like *comedies*.

Expressing Dislikes

I don't like to *run*.

I don't like *comedies* very much.

Intention

Inquiring about . . .

What are you going to do *this weekend*?

Expressing . . .

I'm going to *paint my apartment*.

Obligation

Expressing . . .

I have to *work late*.

Advice-Suggestions

Offering . . .

Let's *do something outdoors today*.

Ability/Inability

Expressing Inability

I'm afraid I can't.

Disappointment

That's too bad.

Leave Taking

Have a good weekend!
    You, too.

Satisfaction/Dissatisfaction

Inquiring about . . .

Did you enjoy it?

Expressing Satisfaction

Yes. It was excellent.

Conversation Strategy

Checking and Indicating Understanding

Checking One's Own Understanding

Tonight?

CHAPTER 10

Functions

Asking for and Reporting Information

Tell me, _____?

What's *your major*?
Where *are you from*?
Why *are you here*?
Which *apartment do you live in*?

And you?

Can I ask you a question?

Is there *a laundromat in the neighborhood*?
    There's *a laundromat around the corner*.

I was in *Detroit*.
    What did you do *there*?
I *visited my daughter and her husband*.

What are you doing?

What's wrong with *it*?
What's the problem?
    It's *leaking*.

Do you *fix kitchen sinks*?

What's the name?
    Eric Jensen.
Spell the last name, please.
    J-E-N-S-E-N.
And the address?
    93 Cliff Street.
Phone number?
    972-3053.

Greeting People

Hello.
Hi.

Nice to meet you.
    Nice meeting you, too.

Attracting Attention

Excuse me.
Pardon me.

Gratitude

Expressing . . .

Thank you.
Thanks.
Thanks very much.

Appreciation

I appreciate it.

Introductions

Introducing Oneself

I'm *your neighbor*.

My name is *Helen*.
I'm *Maria*.

Permission

Inquiring about Permissibility

Can I *park my car here*?

Indicating Permissibility

Yes, you can.

No, you can't.

Offering to Help

Making an Offer

Can I help you *take out the garbage*?

Let me help you.

Responding to an Offer

No. That's okay.

Well, all right.

If you don't mind.

Thanks. I appreciate it.

Persuading-Insisting

Please.

Requests

Direct, Polite

Could I ask you a favor?

Could you *lend me a hammer*?

Responding to Requests

All right.

I'd be happy to *lend you a hammer*.

Advice-Suggestions

Offering . . .

Maybe you should *call a plumber*.

May I ask *who's calling?*

What's your name?
  Edward Bratt.

I'm afraid *she* isn't here right now.
  When will *she* be back?
She'll probably be back *in an hour.*

When is the next *bus to Buffalo?*
  It's at *4:10.*

That'll be *twenty-four dollars and fifty cents.*

I want to report an emergency!

A car just hit a pedestrian.

Instructing

Dial "one." Dial the area code. Then, *dial the local phone number.*

Identifying

Operator.
Police.

This is *her friend Steve.*

Requests

Direct, Polite

Please *fasten your seat belt.*

Please ask *her* to call *me.*

Responding to Requests

All right.
Oh, okay.

Attracting Attention

Excuse me.

Gratitude

Expressing . . .

Thanks very much.

Want-Desire

Inquiring about . . .

Do you want to *leave a message?*

Expressing . . .

I want to *make this a collect call,* please.

I'd like *a round-trip ticket,* please.

Correcting

Giving Correction

No. *Edward Bratt.*

Probability/Improbability

Expressing Probability

She'll probably *be back in an hour.*

Directions-Location

Inquiring about Location

Where?

Giving Location

At the corner of *Broadway and K Street.*
In front of *the Hilton Hotel.*
In *the parking lot* on *Maple Street.*
Near *the statue of Robert E. Lee.*
On *Washington Street* between *Second and Third Avenue.*

Conversation Strategies

Checking and Indicating Understanding

Checking Another Person's Understanding

Have you got it?

Checking One's Own Understanding

Let me see.

Did you say *Edward Pratt?*

At 4:10?

Indicating Understanding

Okay.
I understand.
Oh, I see.

Asking for Repetition

Could you repeat the last step?

I'm sorry. I didn't hear you. What did you say?

Initiating Conversations

May I please speak to *Betty?*

CHAPTER 13

Functions

Want-Desire

Inquiring about . . .

What would you like?

Would you like *anything to drink?*
Do you want *anything to drink?*

What do you want me to *get?*

Expressing . . .

I want *a pound of roast beef.*
I'd like *a hamburger.*
I'll have *a cup of coffee.*

We need *a few things from the supermarket.*

Complimenting

Expressing Compliments

It's/They're
$\begin{cases} \text{delicious.} \\ \text{very good.} \\ \text{excellent.} \\ \text{fantastic.} \end{cases}$

Your *cake* was delicious.

Requests

Direct, Polite

Could you do me a favor?

Responding to Requests

Sure.

Preference

Inquiring about . . .

Would you prefer *rice* or *a baked potato?*

Expressing . . .

I'd prefer *a baked potato.*

Instructing

First, *mix together a cup of flour, a teaspoon of salt, and two tablespoons of water.*
Then, *add half a cup of sugar.*
Next, *add two eggs.*
And then, *put the mixture into a baking pan.*

Persuading-Insisting

Oh, come on!

Asking for and Reporting Information

Do we need *anything from the supermarket?*
   Yes. We need *a quart of milk.*

That'll be *seven twenty-five.*
That comes to *two dollars and ninety cents.*

Your change is *two dollars and seventy-five cents.*

Can you tell me *the recipe?*

Intention

Expressing . . .

I'll *get a quart of milk.*

Gratitude

Thank you.
Thanks.

Offering to Help

Making an Offer

May I help you?

Leave Taking

Have a nice day.

Greeting People

Welcome to *Burger King.*

Conversation Strategies

Checking and Indicating Understanding

Checking Another Person's Understanding

Are you with me so far?

Have you got all that?

Checking One's Own Understanding

A quart?
Seven twenty-five?

A can of tuna fish, a loaf of white bread, and a head of lettuce.

That's *a pound of roast beef and a dozen rolls.*
Okay. That's *a hamburger, an order of french fries, and a cup of coffee.*

Indicating Understanding

I see.
Uh-húh.
I'm following you.
I've got it.

Hesitating

Let me see . . .

CHAPTER 14

Functions

Remembering/Forgetting

Inquiring about . . .

Did you remember to *pay the telephone bill?*

Do you remember *the amount?*

Did I forget to *print my name on the deposit slip?*

Indicating . . .

I forgot.
I forgot to *tell you.*

Reminding . . .

Remember . . . *We have to buy stamps.*

Describing

It's very *large.*

It's *larger* than *that one.*

It's the *firmest mattress* in *the store.*

Agreement/Disagreement

Expressing Agreement

I know.
You're right.
I think so, too.

I suppose not.

Certainty/Uncertainty

Inquiring about . . .

Are you sure?

Expressing Certainty

I'm positive.

I think *there's a mistake on my electric bill.*
I believe *I was charged too much.*

Advice-Suggestions

Asking for . . .

How much do you think *we should get?*

Offering . . .

I think *we* should *stop at the bank.*

I think *forty dollars will be enough.*

You should *ask for your money back.*

Preference

Inquiring about . . .

Which *refrigerator* do you like?

Expressing . . .

I like *this one.*

Offering to Help

Making an Offer

May I help you?

Want-Desire

Expressing . . .

I'm looking for *a firm mattress.*

I'd like to *deposit this in my savings account.*

Asking for and Reporting Information

How much is it?
   Three hundred dollars.

Why *are you banging on the vending machine?*

What is your name?
   John Lawson.
And your account number?
   463 21 0978.
And what is the amount on your bill?
   Four hundred and thirty dollars.

Requests

Direct, Polite

Can you *show me a less expensive one?*

Please *print your name on the deposit slip.*

Responding to Requests

Certainly.

I'll be happy to.

Obligation

Expressing . . .

We have to *buy stamps.*

Intention

Expressing . . .

I will.

We're going to *take the kids to the zoo tomorrow.*

Apologizing

Sorry.

Gratitude

Expressing . . .

Thank you.
Thanks.

Sympathizing

That's too bad!

Identifying

Southeast Electric Company.

Conversation Strategies

Checking and Indicating Understanding

Checking One's Own Understanding

The telephone bill?

Indicating Understanding

I see.

Initiating a Topic

You know . . .

CHAPTER 15

Functions

Correcting

Giving Correction

You aren't *bagging the groceries* the right way.

You're supposed to *attach the black wire to the switch.*
You've got to *put the eggs on top.*

No, not exactly.

Responding to Correction

Oh, I see. Thank you.

Oh. I didn't know that.

Thanks for telling me.

Approval/Disapproval

Inquiring about . . .

Am I *assembling this computer* correctly?

Am I *working fast* enough?

Expressing Approval

You're *typing* very *accurately.*

Expressing Disapproval

Actually, you should try to *work faster.*

Obligation

Expressing . . .

You're supposed to *attach the black wire to the switch.*
You've got to *put the eggs on top.*

Warning

Be careful!
Careful!
Look out!
Watch it!
Watch out!

Put on your safety glasses!
Don't *stand there!*

Advice-Suggestions

Offering . . .

You should *try to work faster.*

I think *we* should *put a juice machine in the employee lounge.*

May I offer a suggestion?

Responding to . . .

Thanks for telling me.
Thanks for the suggestion.

I'll think about it.

Why do you suggest that?

Complimenting

Expressing Compliments

You're a very *accurate typist!*

Responding to Compliments

Thank you for saying so.

Do you really think so?

Promising

Offering a Promise

I promise *I'll turn them off.*

Attracting Attention

Excuse me. *Mr. Johnson?*
Excuse me, *Mr. Mitchell.*
Jimmy?

Possibility/Impossibility

Expressing Possibility

You might *hurt yourself.*

Gratitude

Expressing . . .

Thanks for *the warning.*

Asking for and Reporting Information

Tony is hurt!
   What happened?
He burned himself on the stove.

Instructing

Tell *him* to *put cold water on the burn*.

Intention

Expressing . . .

I'll *get the first-aid kit*.

Requests

Direct, Polite

Will you *turn off the lights when you leave?*

Responding to Requests

Yes, I will.

Remembering/Forgetting

Reminding

Please don't forget.

Agreement/Disagreement

Expressing Agreement

You might be right.

Conversation Strategies

Checking and Indicating Understanding

Checking One's Own Understanding

I'm not?

Asking for Repetition

Excuse me?

CHAPTER 16

Functions

Permission

Inquiring about Permissibility

Are you allowed to *swim here?*

Indicating Permissibility

Yes, you are.
No, you aren't.

You aren't allowed to *park here*.
I don't think you're allowed to *hang your clothes there*.
Tenants aren't permitted to *hang laundry on the balcony*.

Asking for and Reporting Information

May I ask you a question?

Tell me, _____?

What's the matter?

What did I do wrong?
You *went through a red light*.

What did the sign say?

Why do you say that?

It's a legal holiday.

Surprise-Disbelief

Oh, my goodness!
Oops!
Uh-oh!

"*No Right Turn on Red*"?!
A red light?

Promising

Offering a Promise

I promise I'll *fix your sink this week*.

Attracting Attention

Excuse me.
Excuse me, but *I don't think you're allowed to hang your clothes there*.

Gratitude

Expressing . . .

Thank you.
Thank you very much.
Thanks for *telling me*.

Responding to . . .

You're welcome.

Apologizing

Sorry.

Granting Forgiveness

That's okay.

Identifying

Hello. This is *Mr. Grant* in *Apartment 2*.

Intention

Inquiring about . . .

When are you going to *fix my sink?*

Expressing . . .

I'll *try to fix it soon*.

I will.

Obligation

Inquiring about . . .

Do I have to *work on July 4th?*

Advice-Suggestions

Offering . . .

You should *write to the mayor*.
You ought to *write to the mayor*.

Responding to . . .

That's a good idea.

Conversation Strategies

Focusing Attention

You know, *you promised to fix it several weeks ago*.

In my opinion, *they should have more buses on this route*.

Checking and Indicating Understanding

Checking One's Own Understanding

Write to the mayor?

Indicating Understanding

I see.

Initiating a Topic

You know . . .

CHAPTER 17

Functions

Asking for and Reporting Information

What's new with you?
  Nothing much. How about you?

I have some good news.
I have some bad news.
  Really? What?

Did you see *the "Phil Crosby Show" last night?*
Did you *do anything special over the weekend?*

What happened?

Where did you hear that?
  I heard it *in the cafeteria.*
  One of the secretaries told me.
  They talked about it *at a union meeting.*
  I overhead it *on the elevator.*
  Everybody *in the office* is talking
    about it.

Who *cut it?*
What *is her name?*
When *did you get it?*
Where *did you buy them?*
Why *are you wearing it?*
Which *game did you see?*
How *does it ride?*

Complimenting

Expressing Compliments

I like *your new car.*

It's very *fancy.*

Responding to Compliments

Thank you.

Satisfaction/Dissatisfaction

Inquiring about . . .

Did you enjoy it?

Expressing Satisfaction

We enjoyed it a lot.

Congratulating

That's great!
Congratulations!

Sympathizing

That's too bad!
I'm sorry to hear that.

Correcting

Giving Correction

No. *Fries.*

Gratitude

Expressing . . .

Thank you.
Thanks.

Surprise-Disbelief

Really?

I can't believe it!
I'm really surprised.

Likes/Dislikes

Expressing Likes

I like *your new car.*

Describing

It was very *funny.*

Regret

I'm sorry *I missed it.*

Intention

Inquiring about . . .

What are you going to do *on your next day off?*

Certainty/Uncertainty

Expressing Uncertainty

I'm not sure.
I don't know.

I'm not sure yet.

Probability/Improbability

Expressing Probability

I'll probably *clean my apartment.*

Possibility/Impossibility

Expressing Possibility

I might *go to a museum.*
Maybe I'll *visit my parents.*

Wish-Hope

I hope *you enjoy yourself.*

Conversation Strategies

Checking and Indicating Understanding

Checking One's Own Understanding

Did you say *pies?*

Indicating Understanding

Oh. I understand.

Initiating a Topic

What's new with you?

Did you hear the news?

Interrupting

Excuse me.

I'm sorry to interrupt, but *we're out of fries.*

Clarification

Asking for Clarification

I'm afraid I'm not following you.
What does that mean?

Giving Clarification

What that means is *they aren't working right now.*

CHAPTER 18

Functions

Agreement/Disagreement

Inquiring about . . .

Don't you agree?
Don't you think so?

Expressing Agreement

I agree.
You're right.

Maybe you're right.

I was thinking the same thing.

Expressing Disagreement

I disagree.
I'm not so sure.

Leave Taking

I've really got to go now.

I think I should be going now.
  I should be going, too.

Good-bye.
Bye.
Bye-bye.

So long.
See you soon.
Take it easy.
Take care.

I'll call you soon.

Obligation

Expressing . . .

I've got to *go now.*
I have to *get back to work.*

Asking for and Reporting Information

Tell me, _____?

How *is David doing in Math this year?*

*Michael started a fight in the school
  cafeteria this morning.*

I think *this bread is stale.*

Why do you say that?
What makes you say that?

What time is it?
  It's *1:30.*

Introductions

Introducing Oneself

Hello. I'm *Mrs. Carter.*

Greeting People

I'm pleased to meet you.
  Nice to meet you, too.

Hello. Is this *Mr. Johnson?*

Approval/Disapproval

Expressing Approval

He's doing very well.
He works very *hard.*
His grades are excellent.

You should be very proud of *him.*

Gratitude

Expressing . . .

Thank you.
Thank you for *letting me know.*

Responding to . . .

You're welcome.

Identifying

This is *Mrs. Smith, the school principal,*
  calling.

Surprise-Disbelief

Oh!

He did?

It's late!

Promising

Offering a Promise

I promise I'll *speak to him.*

Advice-Suggestions

Offering . . .

We should *have a party for her.*
We should probably *close the pool.*
Maybe we should *do them again.*

We probably shouldn't *bother him.*

Conversation Strategies

Initiating a Topic

You know . . . *the boss is in a terrible
  mood today.*

Focusing Attention

In my opinion, *English is a very difficult
  language.*

TOPIC VOCABULARY GLOSSARY

The number after each word indicates the page where the word first appears.

(n) = noun
(v) = verb

Banking

account number 143
amount 143
cash *this* check 143
check (n) 143
checking account 143
deposit (v) 143
deposit slip 143
endorse 143
make a withdrawal 143
print *your name* 143
savings account 143
sign *your name* 143
withdrawal slip 143

Citizen Participation

call (v) 169
city manager 169
congressman 169
congresswoman 169
express *your* opinion 169
governor 169
mayor 169
newspaper 169
President 169
radio talk show 169
senator 169
send a letter 169
speak 169
town meeting 169
write to 169

Clothing

belt 63
blouse 62
boots 66
coat 62
dress 62
earrings 66
gloves 64
hat 62
jacket 64
jeans 67
necklace 66
pajamas 67
pants 62
purse 67
raincoat 63
shirt 62
shoes 62
skirt 64
sneakers 64
socks 63
stockings 66
suit 64
sweater 63
tie (n) 62
umbrella 62
watch (n) 66

Coins

penny – 1 cent 145
nickel – 5 cents 145
dime – 10 cents 145
quarter – 25 cents 145

Colors

black 63
blue 63
brown 63
gray 63
green 63
red 63
white 63
yellow 63

Community

airport 13
bank 12
beach 30
bus station 18
bus stop 99
clinic 12
department store 22
drug store 18
fire station 19
gas station 19
grocery store 19
hospital 19
hotel 19
laundromat 12
library 12
mail 99
mall 13
movies (movie theater) 13
museum 13
park (n) 12
parking lot 19
police station 19
post office 12
school 12
shopping mall 23
supermarket 12
theater 24
train station 23
university 30
zoo 13

Countries

China 6
Egypt 6
Italy 6
Japan 6
Mexico 6
The Soviet Union 6

Days of the Week 41

Sunday
Monday
Tuesday
Wednesday
Thursday
Friday
Saturday

Department Store

aisle 62
basement 65
bedroom furniture 65
camera 66
cassette player 141
computer 140
counter 62
Customer Service
    Counter 65
dressing room 65
elevator 65
fan 67
price 66
rack 62
radio 65
receipt 67
refrigerator 65
refund (n) 67
rest rooms 65
sale 66
stereo system 140
tax (n) 66
textbook 67
TV 65
typewriter 66
videogame 67

Describing

attractive 140
beautiful 176
big 64
comfortable 140
delicious 136
difficult 67
dramatic 177
easy 67
excellent 136
exciting 177
expensive 140
fancy 176
fantastic 136
firm 141
friendly 176
funny 177
good 140
heavy 67
interesting 177
large 64
lightweight 141

long 64
nice 140
noisy 67
powerful 140
quiet 140
scary 177
short 64
small 63
stylish 176
tight 64
very good 136

Describing People

height 73
    very tall 73
    tall 73
    average height 73
    short 73
    very short 73
weight 73
    very thin 73
    thin 73
    heavy 73
    very heavy 73
hair 73
    black 73
    blond/blonde 73
    brown 73
    curly 73
    dark 73
    gray 73
    light 73
    red 73
    straight 73

Driving

Do Not Enter 164
drive (v) 165
drive through *a stop
    sign* 165
go *90 miles per hour* 165
go through *a red light* 165
illegal 165
license 165
make *an illegal U* turn 165
90 miles per hour 165
No Left Turn 164
No Right Turn on Red 164
No U Turn 164
Officer 165
One Way 164
red light 165
road 165
speed (v) 165
Stop 164
stop sign 165
ticket 165
U turn 165
wrong side of the road 165

IRREGULAR VERBS

be	was/were		lose	lost
bleed	bled		make	made
break	broke		mean	meant
buy	bought		meet	met
catch	caught		overhear	overheard
come	came		pay	paid
cut	cut		put	put
do	did		quit	quit
drive	drove		read	read
eat	ate		ride	rode
fall	fell		ring	rang
feed	fed		run	ran
feel	felt		say	said
find	found		see	saw
fit	fit		send	sent
forget	forgot		set	set
get	got		sit	sat
give	gave		speak	spoke
go	went		stand	stood
hang	hung		steal	stole
have	had		sweep	swept
hear	heard		swim	swam
hit	hit		take	took
hold	held		teach	taught
hurt	hurt		tell	told
keep	kept		think	thought
know	knew		throw	threw
lay	laid		understand	understood
leave	left		wear	wore
lend	lent		write	wrote
lie	lay			

INDEX OF FUNCTIONS AND CONVERSATION STRATEGIES

INDEX OF TOPICS

INDEX OF GRAMMATICAL STRUCTURES